100 More Afghan Squares to Knit

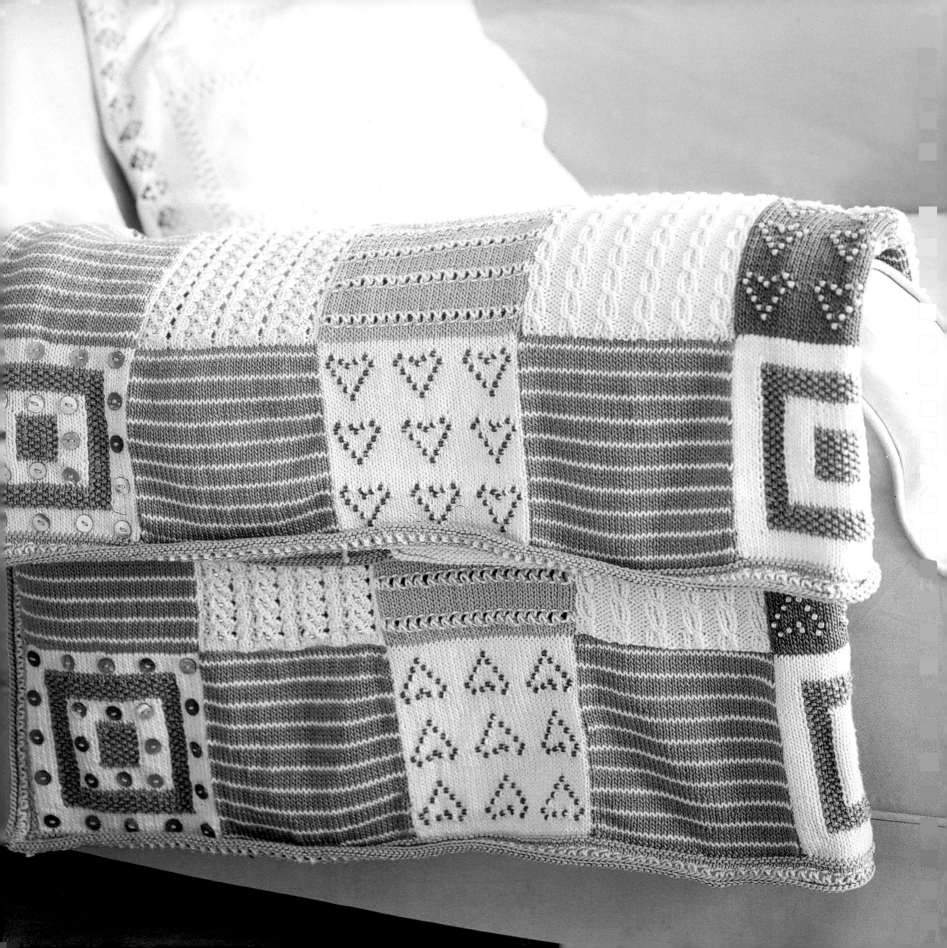

100 More Afghan Squares to Knit

Debbie Abrahams

Trafalgar Square Publishing

North Pomfret, Vermont

First published in the United States of America in 2005
by Trafalgar Square Publishing
North Pomfret, Vermont 05053

Printed and bound in Singapore by Kyodo Printing Co Pte Ltd

1 3 5 7 9 8 6 4 2

Edited and designed by Collins & Brown Limited
EDITOR: Emma Callery
DESIGNER: HL Studios
PHOTOGRAPHY: Michael Wicks
COVER PHOTOGRAPH: Sandra Lane
PATTERN CHECKING: Marilyn Wilson
ILLUSTRATIONS: Luise Roberts

Library of Congress Control Number: 2005905035
ISBN-13: 978-1-57076-322-9
ISBN-10: 1-57076-322-4

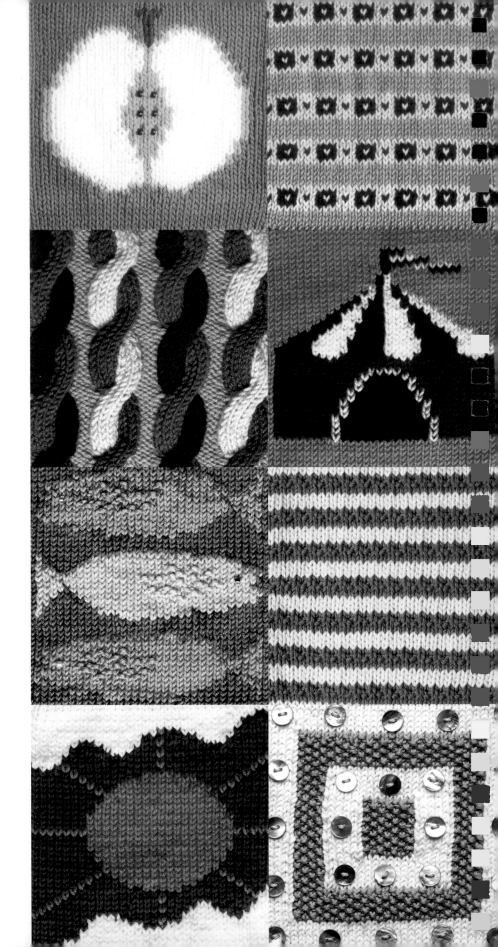

Contents

During my travels around the UK and USA I have been encouraged by the amount of people who are returning to the craft or who are picking up knitting needles for the first time. More and more people of all ages can be seen knitting in all sorts of places – on the bus, on the train, during lunch breaks and even in pubs and clubs! This resurgence of interest in the craft is due to several factors. The influence of modern technology has had a beneficial effect, with exciting colors and fibers readily available in the yarn stores. There is also a huge choice of well-designed knitting patterns on offer, giving knitters the opportunity to create something exclusive and special for themselves. The media has also helped to raise the profile of hand-knitting by promoting it as something hip and fashionable to do in your spare time, which has enticed pop stars and movie stars to take an interest in the craft. It is also possible to see knitting as a welcome antidote to the rush of modern living, bringing a calming influence to bear, a therapeutic relaxation.

With all of this in mind, I have put together in this book a range of knitting projects, which can be successfully created by knitters of all abilities and ages. For example, Big and Cozy (page 9) is an easy-to-knit design that any knitter could enjoy, while for the more experienced knitter the colorful imagery of The Four Seasons (page 109) would provide an appetizing challenge. For this collection I have selected themes that I feel will fit with today's trends and at the same time provide opportunities for personal development and interpretation.

A comment often made to me in my workshops on both sides of the Atlantic is that the finished afghans knitted from my designs are seen as heirlooms, to be kept and treasured in the family for years to come, perhaps even for grandchildren to enjoy. So here in my second book of afghan designs, I offer twelve more projects for you to enjoy, creating furnishings that will be a source of pleasure for many years to come.

Debbie Abrahams

How to use this book

Each separate square has full instructions, either in the form of a written pattern or a chart. In addition there is a color photograph of every square, with some squares having additional photographs showing different colorways. Each chart has a key next to it, and below is a summary of the various symbols used, both in the charts and with the patterns. Before you start a square, check to see if it has a chart, a photograph or both.

In addition there is a techniques section starting on page 119 that has step-by-step instructions for intarsia knitting (the technique used for some of the squares), bead and sequin knitting, embroidery and piecing your afghan.

Key

⊞ Square is charted

▣ Square is illustrated with a photograph

☐ K on RS, P on WS

⊟ P on RS, K on WS

☉ Place bead

☒ Place button

big and cozy

The theme for this easy-to-knit afghan is comfort and warmth, which is achieved through the combination of a soft, chunky yarn with oversized textured stitches. Cables, bobbles and seed stitch patterns make up the basic squares for this design. The theme of comfort and warmth is further enhanced by the choice of colors—orange and red tweed. The squares are quick and easy-to-knit with the chunky yarn, making this a good project for a beginner.

SIZE

73½in × 73½in (184cm × 184cm)

MATERIALS

1 pair US 10.5 (7.00mm/No. 2)
   needles
2 circular US 10.5 (6.5mm/No. 3)
   needles 39in (100cm length)
Cable needle

Yarn

Rowan Plaid
3½oz (100g) balls
   red tweed   23
   orange tweed   12

Quantities given for individual squares are approximate fractions of a ball.

GAUGE (TENSION)

12 sts and 18 rows to 4in (10cm) measured over stockinette (stocking) stitch using US 10.5 (7.00mm/No. 2) needles.

ABBREVIATIONS

See page 127.

FINISHING

The sizes given for the finished afghan and individual squares are approximate. The number of stitches in a row, and the number of rows in a square differ in some instances. Therefore, when sewing pieces together, ease the extra stitches or rows into the adjoining square.

Press the individual squares using a damp cloth and a warm iron. Sew the squares together, joining bound (cast) off edge of one square to the cast-on edge of the next square, easing in stitches, if necessary, to form vertical strips. Sew the vertical strips together, easing in rows, if necessary, to create one block.

Edging

MATERIALS

2 circular US 10.5 (6.5mm/No. 3)
   needles 39ln (100cm) length

Yarn

Rowan Plaid
3½oz (100g) balls
   red tweed   2

KNIT

With RS facing, pick up and knit 254 sts along the RH edge of the afghan.
Beg with a WS row, cont to work in garter stitch (knit every row) for 5 rows, inc 1 st at each end of all WS rows.
Bind (cast) off sts purlwise.
Rep for LH edge of the afghan.
With RS facing, pick up and knit 251 sts along bottom edge of the afghan.
Rep edging as for RH and LH edges.
Rep for top edge of afghan.
Neatly sew border edges together.

Order of squares

QUANTITY OF SQUARES

① Big and cozy cable   12
② Zigzag   12
③ Chunky textured stripe   12
④ Large bobble check   5
⑤ The big twist   4
⑥ Chunky rib   4

❶ Big and cozy cable

SIZE
10½in × 10½in (26cm × 26cm)

MATERIALS
1 pair US 10.5 (7.00mm/No. 2) needles
Cable needle

Single colorway (× 12 ◼)
Rowan Plaid
3½oz (100g) balls
    red tweed   ⁴/₅

KNIT
Cast on 38 sts.
ROW 1 (RS) (INC): P3, [(K1, inc once into next st) 4 times, P4] twice, (K1, inc once into next st) 4 times, P3 *(50 sts)*.
ROW 2 (WS): K3, (P12, K4) twice, P12, K3.
ROW 3 (RS): P3, (K12, P4) twice, K12, P3.
ROW 4 (WS): As row 2.
ROWS 5–10: Rep rows 3–4, 3 times.
ROW 11 (RS): P3, (c12b, P4) twice, c12b, P3.
ROW 12 (WS): As row 2.
ROWS 13–26: Rep rows 3–4, 7 times.
Rep rows 11–26 once more.
Rep rows 11–17 once more.
NEXT ROW (WS) (DEC): K3, [(P1, P2tog) 4 times, K4] twice, (P1, P2tog) 4 times, K3 *(38 sts)*.
(50 rows) Bind (cast) off sts.

❷ Zigzag

SIZE
10½in × 10½in (26cm × 26cm)

Single colorway (× 12 ▣)

MATERIALS
1 pair US 10.5 (7.00mm/No. 2)
needles

Rowan Plaid
3½oz (100g) balls
    orange tweed   ³/₅

KNIT
Cast on 37 sts.
ROW 1 (RS): Knit.
ROW 2 (WS): Purl.
ROW 3 (RS): K3, (P1, K5) 5 times,
P1, K3.
ROW 4 (WS): P2, (K1, P1, K1, P3) 5
times, K1, P1, K1, P2.
ROW 5 (RS): K1, (P1, K1) 18 times.
ROW 6 (WS): K1, (P1, K1) 18 times.
ROW 7 (RS): K1, P1, (K3, P1, K1, P1)
5 times, K3, P1, K1.
ROW 8 (WS): K1, (P5, K1) 6 times.
ROWS 9–10: Rep rows 1–2 once.
ROW 11 (RS): P1, (K5, P1) 6 times.
ROW 12 (WS): P1, K1, (P3, K1, P1,
K1) 5 times, P3, K1, P1.
ROW 13 (RS): P1, (K1, P1) 18 times.
ROW 14 (WS): P1, (K1, P1) 18 times.
ROW 15 (RS): K2, (P1, K1, P1, K3) 5
times, P1, K1, P1, K2.
ROW 16 (WS): P3, (K1, P5) 5 times,
K1, P3.
Rep rows 1–16 twice more.
Rep rows 1–2 once more.
(50 rows).
Bind (cast) off sts.

❸ Chunky textured stripe

SIZE
10½in × 10½in (26cm × 26cm)

MATERIALS
1 pair US 10.5 (7.00mm/No. 2) needles

Single colorway (x 12■)
Rowan Plaid
3½oz (100g) balls
    orange tweed (A)   ⅓
    red tweed (B)   ⅓

KNIT
Cast on 37 sts using A.
Note: Do not cut off yarns. Carry them up the side of the work.
ROW 1 (RS): **A, knit.**
ROW 2 (WS): **A, purl.**
ROW 3 (RS): **B, knit.**
ROW 4 (WS): **B, purl.**
ROW 5 (RS): **K1A, (P1A, K1A) 18 times.**
ROW 6 (WS): **A, purl.**
ROW 7 (RS): **K2B, (P1B, K1B) 17 times, K1B.**
ROW 8 (WS): **B, purl.**
Rep rows 5–8 once more.
Rep rows 1–12, 3 times more.
Rep rows 1–2 once more.
(50 rows)
Bind (cast) off sts.

❹ Large bobble check

SIZE
10½in × 10½in (26cm × 26cm)

MATERIALS
1 pair US 10.5 (7.00mm/No. 2) needles

Single colorway (x 5■)
Rowan Plaid
3½oz (100g) balls
    red tweed   ⁷⁄₁₀

KNIT
Cast on 37 sts.
ROW 1 (RS): **P6, (K5, P5) 3 times, P1.**
ROW 2 (WS): **K6, (P5, K5) 3 times, K1.**
ROWS 3–4: **Rep rows 1–2.**
ROW 5 (RS): **P3, mb, P2, (K5, P2, mb, P2) 3 times, P1.**
ROW 6 (WS): **As row 2.**
ROW 7 (RS): **As row 1.**
ROW 8 (WS): **P6, (K5, P5) 3 times, P1.**
ROW 9 (RS): **K6, (P5, K5) 3 times, K1.**
ROWS 10–11: **Rep rows 8–9.**
Break off yarn.
Transfer sts back onto LH needle, so that the RS is facing you again. Re-join yarn.
ROW 12 (RS): **K6, (P2, mb, P2, K5) 3 times, K1.**
ROWS 13–14: **Rep rows 8–9.**
Break off yarn.
Transfer sts back onto LH needle, so that the RS is facing you again. Re-join yarn.
Rep rows 1–14 twice more.
Rep rows 1–7 once more.
(49 rows)
Bind (cast) off sts.

❺ The big twist

SIZE
10½in × 10½in (26cm × 26cm)

MATERIALS
1 pair US 10.5 (7.00mm/No. 2) needles

Cable needle

Single colorway (x 4■)
Rowan Plaid
3½oz (100g) balls
red tweed   17/20

KNIT
Cast on 39 sts.

ROW 1 (RS) (INC): P3, (Inc once into next st, K1, inc once into each of next 2 sts, K1, inc once into next st, P3) 4 times (55 sts).

ROW 2 (WS): K3, [(P1, K1) twice, P2, (K1, P1) twice, K3] 4 times.

ROW 3 (RS): P3, [(K1, P1) twice, K2, (P1, K1) twice, P3] 4 times.

ROW 4 (WS): Rep row 2.

ROWS 5–8: Rep rows 3–4 twice more.

ROW 9 (RS): P3, [sl next 5 sts onto cable needle and hold at front of work, (K1, P1) twice, K1, then (K1, P1) twice, K1 from cable needle, P3] 4 times.

ROW 10 (WS): As row 2.

ROWS 11–20: Rep rows 3–4, 5 times more.

ROW 21 (RS): P3, [sl next 5 sts onto cable needle and hold at back of work, (K1, P1) twice, K1, then (K1, P1) twice, K1 from cable needle, P3] 4 times.

ROW 22 (WS): As row 2.

ROWS 23–32: Rep rows 3–4, 5 times.

Rep rows 9–25 once more.

NEXT ROW (WS) (DEC): K3, [P2tog, P1, (P2tog) twice, P1, P2tog, K3] 4 times (39 sts).

(50 rows)

Bind (cast) off sts.

❻ Chunky rib

SIZE
10½in × 10½in (26cm × 26cm)

MATERIALS
1 pair US 10.5 (7.00mm/No. 2) needles

Single colorway (x 4■)
Rowan Plaid
3½oz (100g) balls
red tweed   3/5

KNIT
Cast on 37 sts.

ROW 1 (RS): P2, [(K1, P1) twice, K1, P2] 5 times.

ROW 2 (WS): K2, [(P1, K1) twice, P1, K2] 5 times.

ROW 3 (RS): P2, [(yb, sl1p, yf, P1) twice, yb, sl1p, P2] 5 times.

ROW 4 (WS): As row 2.

Rep rows 3–4, 25 times more.

(54 rows)

Bind (cast) off sts.

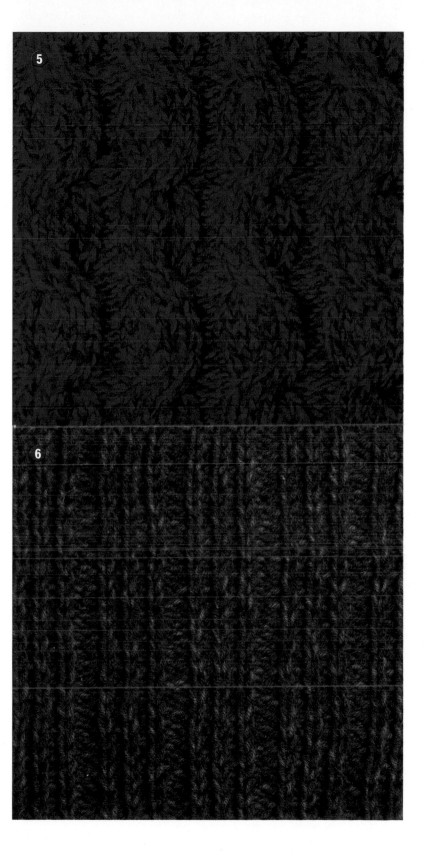

denim hearts

A sister afghan to Queen of Hearts, which appeared in my previous book, this same theme has been re-worked here, this time in denim yarn. I have returned to a favorite motif of mine, the heart, with its connotations of warmth, affection and the home. It is immediately recognizable and capable of many adaptations. In this design I have used this concept to establish a feeling of ease and well-being. Denim yarn has the unique property of fading after washing, giving the look of traditional denim fabric. The three shades of blue yarn are combined with pearl and ruby red beads, which add sparkle to the design and combine well with the various stitch textures.

SIZE
91in × 63in (228cm × 158cm)

MATERIALS
1 pair US 6 (4.00mm/No. 8)
  needles
2 circular US 3 (3.25mm/No. 10)
  needles 39in (100cm) length
Cable needle

Yarn
Rowan Denim
1¾oz (50g) balls

dark denim blue	20
mid denim blue	20
light denim blue	22

Quantities given for individual squares are approximate fractions of a ball.

Beads
³⁄₁₆in (5mm) beads

red	2465
pearl	1244

GAUGE (TENSION)
(before washing)
20 sts and 28 rows to 4in (10cm) measured over stockinette (stocking) stitch using US 6 (4.00mm/No. 8) needles.

ABBREVIATIONS
See page 127.

FINISHING
The sizes given for the finished afghan and individual squares are approximate. The number of stitches in a row, and the number of rows in a square differ in some instances. Therefore, when sewing pieces together, ease the extra stitches or rows into the adjoining square.

Do not press squares. Sew the squares together, joining bound (cast) off edge of one square to the cast-on edge of the next square, easing in stitches, if necessary, to form vertical strips. Sew the vertical strips together, easing in rows, if necessary, to create one block.

Edging

MATERIALS
2 circular US 3 (3.25mm/No. 10) needles 39in (100cm) length

Yarn
Rowan Denim
1¾oz (50g) balls

mid denim blue (A)	1⅙
light denim blue (B)	1⅕
dark denim blue (C)	1⅕

KNIT
With RS facing and using A, pick up and knit 441 sts along the RH edge of the afghan.
Beg with a WS row, work 3 rows in garter stitch (knit every row), inc 1 st at each end of the WS rows (445 sts).
NEXT ROW (RS): B, knit.
NEXT ROW (WS): B, inc once into first st, purl to last 2 sts, inc once into next st, K1 (447 sts).
NEXT ROW (RS): B, knit.
NEXT ROW (WS): C, inc once into first st, purl to last 2 sts, inc once into next st, K1 (449 sts).
NEXT ROW (RS): C, purl.
NEXT ROW (WS): C, inc once into first st, purl to last 2 sts, inc once into next st, K1 (451 sts).
NEXT ROW (RS): C, purl.
Bind (cast) off sts knitwise using B.
Rep for LH edge of the afghan.
With RS facing and using A, pick up and knit 319 sts along bottom edge of the afghan. Rep edging as for RH and LH edges.
Rep for top edge of afghan.
Neatly sew border edges together.

WASHING THE AFGHAN TO ENABLE SHRINKAGE
Denim yarn shrinks when washed. Darn in the ends on the WS of the work. Put the afghan inside a wash bag that can be secured and wash in a large washing machine at a temperature of 70–80°C (or hottest whites wash). Wash separately from other washing. Tumble-dry the afghan for approximately 40 minutes (if facility is available). Re-shape and dry flat.

Order of squares

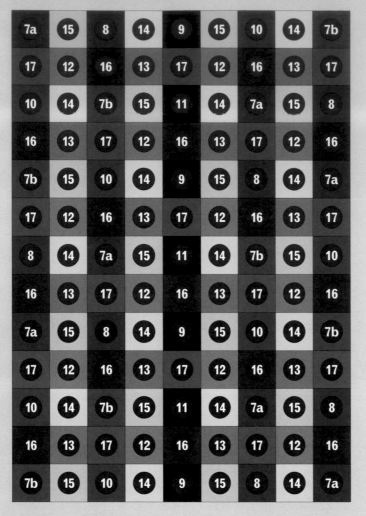

QUANTITY OF SQUARES

⑦ Beaded heart
  - ⑦ₐ First colorway — 7
  - ⑦ᵦ Second colorway — 7
⑧ Patchwork heart — 7
⑨ Bead and texture heart — 4
⑩ Polka dot heart — 7
⑪ Lace heart — 3
⑫ Pearl mini hearts — 12
⑬ Red mini hearts — 12
⑭ Reverse stitch stripe — 14
⑮ Beaded cable — 14
⑯ Basketweave stitch stripe — 15
⑰ Skinny stripe — 15

The squares in this afghan are not suitable for mixing and matching due to the shrinkage of the denim yarn.

❼ Beaded heart

SIZE
7in × 7in (18cm × 18cm)

MATERIALS
1 pair US 6 (4.00mm/No. 8) needles

⑦ₐ First colorway (× 7⊞ ▣)
Rowan Denim
1¾oz (50g) balls
■ dark denim blue   ¼
■ mid denim blue   ⅕

³⁄₁₆in (5mm) beads
● red   119

☐ K on RS, P on WS
⊟ P on RS, K on WS

⑦ᵦ Second colorway (× 7▣)
Rowan Denim
1¾oz (50g) balls
    dark denim blue   ¼
    mid denim blue   ⅕

³⁄₁₆in (5mm) beads
    pearl   59
    red   60

KNIT
First colorway: thread 119 red beads onto yarn.
Second colorway: thread beads onto yarn in the foll sequence:
2 red, 4 pearl, 6 red, 8 pearl, 10 red, 11 pearl, 12 red, 11 pearl, 10 red, 9 pearl, 8 red, 7 pearl, 6 red, 5 pearl, 4 red, 3 pearl, 2 red, 1 pearl.

Cast on 37 sts and work until chart row 58 completed. Bind (cast) off sts.

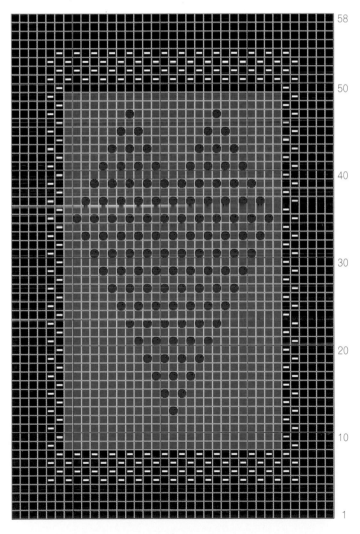

❽ Patchwork heart

SIZE
7in × 7in (18cm × 18cm)

MATERIALS
1 pair US 6 (4.00mm/No. 8) needles

Single colorway (× 7⊞ ▣)
Rowan Denim
1¾oz (50g) balls
■ dark denim blue   ¼
■ mid denim blue   ⅙
■ light denim blue   ¹⁄₁₀
☐ K on RS, P on WS
⊟ P on RS, K on WS
(See chart overleaf)

KNIT
Cast on 37 sts and work until chart row 58 completed. Bind (cast) off sts.

❾ Bead and texture heart

☐ K on RS, P on WS
⊟ P on RS, K on WS

SIZE

7in × 7in (18cm × 18cm)

MATERIALS

1 pair US 6 (4.00mm/No. 8) needles

Single colorway (× 4⊞ ◼)

Rowan Denim
1¾oz (50g) balls
◼ dark denim blue   ¼
◼ mid denim blue   ¼

³⁄₁₆in (5mm) beads
● red   36
◌ pearl   44

KNIT

Thread beads onto yarn in the foll sequence: 7 pearl, 1 red, 2 pearl, 1 red, 2 pearl, 2 red, 2 pearl, 2 red, 2 pearl, 2 red, 2 pearl, 2 red, 2 pearl, 2 red, 1 pearl, 2 red, 2 pearl, 4 red, 2 pearl, 3 red, 2 pearl, 2 red, 2 pearl, 2 red, 2 pearl, 2 red, 2 pearl, 2 red, 2 pearl, 2 red, 2 pearl, 2 red, 2 pearl, 2 red, 2 pearl, 1 red, 4 pearl.
Cast on 37 sts and work until chart row 58 completed.
Bind (cast) off sts.

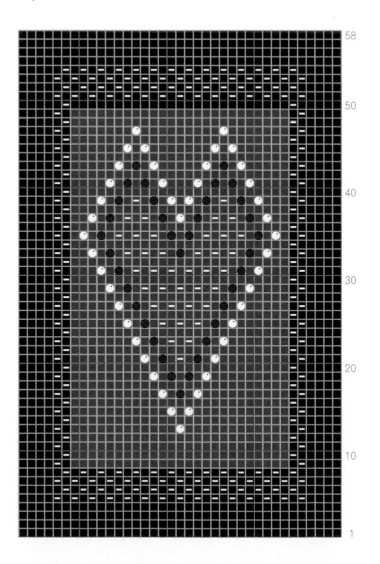

⑩ Polka dot heart

SIZE
7in × 7in (18cm × 18cm)

MATERIALS
1 pair US 6 (4.00mm/No. 8)
   needles

Single colorway (× 7⊞ ▣)
Rowan Denim
1¾oz (50g) balls
■ dark denim blue ¼ plus a small
amount for embroidery
■ mid denim blue   ⅙
■ light denim blue   ⅒

KNIT
Note: Using picture as a guide,
Swiss-darn the polka dots onto
the heart after knitting and before
washing the afghan.

Cast on 37 sts and work until
chart row 58 completed.
Bind (cast) off sts.

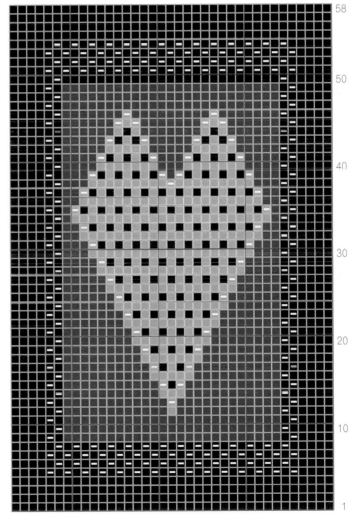

⑪ Lace heart

SIZE
7in × 7in (18cm × 18cm)

MATERIALS
1 pair US 6 (4.00mm/No. 8)
    needles

Single colorway (x 3 ⊞ ▣)
Rowan Denim
1¾oz (50g) balls
■ dark denim blue   ¼
■ mid denim blue   ¼

☐ K on RS, P on WS
⊟ P on RS, K on WS
◪ K2tog
◉ yarn forward

KNIT
Cast on 37 sts and work until
chart row 58 completed.
Bind (cast) off sts.

⑫ Pearl mini hearts

SIZE

7in × 7in (18cm × 18cm)

MATERIALS

1 pair US 6 (4.00mm/No. 8)
   needles

Single colorway (× 12 ⊞ ▣)

Rowan Denim
1³⁄₄oz (50g) balls

■ mid denim blue   ½

³⁄₁₆in (5mm) beads

◌ pearl   54

☐ K on RS, P on WS
⊟ P on RS, K on WS

KNIT

Thread 54 pearl beads onto yarn.

Cast on 37 sts and work until
chart row 59 completed.
Bind (cast) off sts.

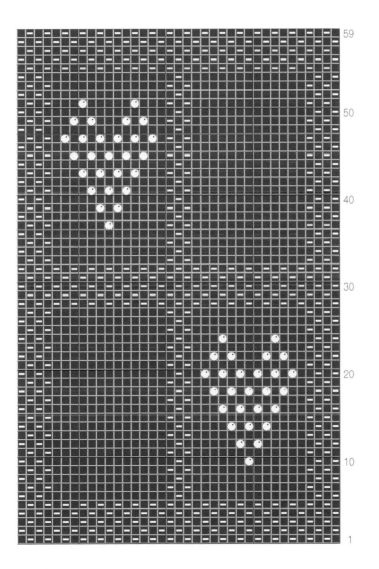

⑬ Red mini hearts

SIZE

7in × 7in (18cm × 18cm)

MATERIALS

1 pair US 6 (4.00mm/No. 8)
   needles

Single colorway (× 12 ⊞ ▣)

Rowan Denim
1³⁄₄oz (50g) balls

■ mid denim blue   ½

³⁄₁₆in (5mm) beads

● red   54

☐ K on RS, P on WS
⊟ P on RS, K on WS

KNIT

Thread 54 red beads onto yarn.

Cast on 37 sts and work until
chart row 59 completed.
Bind (cast) off sts.

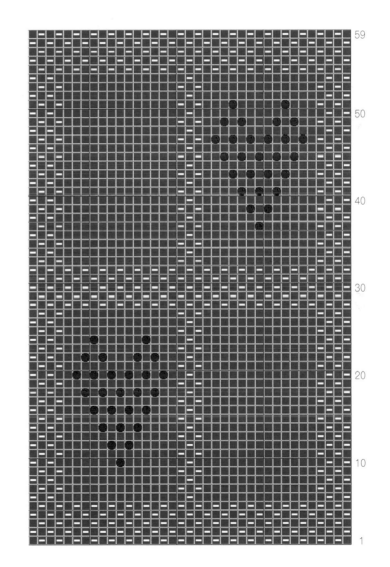

⓮ Reverse stitch stripe

SIZE

7in × 7in (18cm × 18cm)

MATERIALS

1 pair US 6 (4.00mm/No. 8)
    needles

Single colorway (x 14 ■)

Rowan Denim
1¾oz (50g) balls
    light denim blue (A)   ⅕
    dark denim blue (B)   ⅓

KNIT

Cast on 37 sts in the following
sequence: 4A, 5B, 3A, 5B, 3A,
5B, 3A, 5B, 4A.
ROW 1 (RS): (K1A, P1A) twice,
(holding yarns at front of work,
cross yarns over to change to next
color, P5B, holding yarns at front
of work, cross yarns over to
change to next color, P1A, K1A,
P1A) 4 times, K1A.
ROW 2 (WS): (K1A, P1A) twice,
(holding yarns to back of work
between needles, cross yarns over
at back of work to change to next
color, K5B, cross yarns over at
back of work to change color,
bring yarn A forward between
needles, P1A, K1A, P1A) 4 times,
K1A.
Rep these 2 rows, 28 times more.
(58 rows)
Bind (cast) off sts.

⓯ Beaded cable

SIZE

7in × 7in (18cm × 18cm)

MATERIALS

1 pair US 6 (4.00mm/No. 8)
    needles
Cable needle

Single colorway (x 14 ■)

Rowan Denim
1¾oz (50g) balls
    light denim blue   ⁵⁄₇

³⁄₁₆in (5mm) beads
    red   30

KNIT

Thread 30 red beads onto yarn.
Cast on 38 sts.
ROW 1 (RS) (INC): (P2, inc once into
each of the next 3 sts knitwise,
K1) 6 times, P2 (56 sts).
ROW 2 (WS): (K2, P3, K1, P3)
6 times, K2.
ROW 3 (RS): (P2, K3, P1, K3)
6 times, P2.
ROW 4 (WS): (K2, P3, K1, P3)
6 times, K2.
ROW 5 (RS): (P2, sl next 4 sts onto
cable needle and hold at back of
work, K3, sl purl st back onto LH
needle and purl it, K3 from cable
needle) 6 times, P2.
ROW 6 (WS): As row 2.
ROWS 7–9: Rep rows 3–4 once,
then row 3 once more.
ROW 10 (WS): (K2, P3, pb, P3)
6 times, K2.
ROWS 11–14: Rep rows 3–4 twice.
Rep rows 5–14, 4 times more.
Rep rows 5–7 once more.
NEXT ROW (WS) (DEC): [K2, (P2tog)
3 times, P1] 6 times, K2 (38 sts).
(58 rows)
Bind (cast) off sts.

⓰ Basketweave stitch stripe

SIZE

7in × 7in (18cm × 18cm)

MATERIALS

1 pair US 6 (4.00mm/No. 8)
    needles

Single colorway (x 15 ■)

Rowan Denim
1¾oz (50g) balls
    light denim blue (A)   ¼
    dark denim blue (B)   ⅕

KNIT

Cast on 37 sts using A.
ROW 1 (RS): K8A, (P7A, K7A) twice,
K1A.
ROW 2 (WS): P8A, (K7A, P7A) twice,
P1A.
ROWS 3–6: Rep rows 1–2 twice.
ROW 7 (RS): P8B, (K7B, P7B) twice,
P1B.
ROW 8 (WS): K8B, (P7B, K7B)
twice, K1B.
ROWS 9–12: Rep rows 7–8 twice.
Rep rows 1–12, 3 times more.
Rep rows 1–6 once more.
(54 rows)
Bind (cast) off sts.

⓱ Skinny stripe

SIZE

7in × 7in (18cm × 18cm)

MATERIALS

1 pair US 6 (4.00mm/No. 8)
    needles

Single colorway (x 15 ■)

Rowan Denim
1¾oz (50g) balls
    light denim blue (A)   ⅕
    dark denim blue (B)   ¹⁄₁₀
    mid denim blue (C)   ²⁄₂₅

KNIT

Cast on 37 sts using A.
Working in stockinette (stocking)
stitch, cont in stripe patt rep as
folls, beg with a RS row:
ROWS 1–3: A.
ROWS 4–6: B.
ROWS 7–9: A.
ROWS 10–12: C.
Rep rows 1–12, 3 times more.
Rep rows 1–9 once more.
(57 rows)
Bind (cast) off sts.

afternoon tea

China teacups, pastries, and lace tablecloths in a carefully selected palette of fondant colors invoke a feeling of nostalgia. The theme harks back to a former age of elegance but with a contemporary feel through the choice of fresh colors and the reinvention of traditional lace stitches. These intricate stitches, together with beads, hearts, and shell buttons, add textural interest. This afghan complements the English Garden collection in 25 Cushions to Knit. It may appeal to the knitter who wants to move on from basic stitches to something a little more demanding.

SIZE
54in × 54in (135cm × 135cm)

MATERIALS
1 pair US 2–3 (3.00mm/No. 11) needles
2 circular US 2 (2.75mm/No. 12) needles 32ln (80cm) length
Cable needle

Yarn
Rowan Cotton Glace
1³⁄₄oz (50g) balls

cream	14
mld pink	7
purple	3
lilac	2

Quantities given for individual squares are approximate fractions of a ball.

Beads
1⁄8in (3mm) beads

mauve	1512
silver	384
pearl	504

Buttons

Small shell	120

GAUGE (TENSION)
25 sts and 34 rows to 4in (10cm) measured over stockinette (stocking) stitch using US 2–3 (3.00mm/No. 11) needles.

ABBREVIATIONS
See page 127.

FINISHING
The sizes given for the finished afghan and individual squares are approximate. The number of stitches in a row, and the number of rows in a square differ in some instances. Therefore, when sewing pieces together, ease the extra stitches or rows into the adjoining square.

Press the individual squares using a damp cloth and a warm iron. Sew the squares together, joining bound- (cast-) off edge of one square to the cast-on edge of the next square, easing in stitches, if necessary, to form vertical strips. Sew the vertical strips together, easing in rows, if necessary, to create one block.

Edging

MATERIALS

2 circular US 2 (2.75mm/No. 12)
  needles 32in (80cm) length

Yarn

Rowan Cotton Glace
1¾oz (50g) balls
  lilac (A)   1³/₅
  cream (B)   ½

KNIT

With RS facing and using A, pick
up and knit 337 sts along the RH
edge of the afghan.
Beg with a WS row, work as folls:
ROW 1 (WS): A, inc once into the
first st, K to last 2 sts, inc once
into next st, K1 (339 sts).
ROW 2 (RS): A, knit.
ROW 3 (WS): A, inc once into the
first st, P to last 2 sts, inc once
into next st, P1. (341 sts).
ROW 4 (RS): B, K2, (yf, sl1p, yb, K1)
169 times, K1.
ROW 5 (WS): B, inc once into first
st, P1, (yfrn, P2tog) 169 times, inc
once into last st (343 sts).
ROW 6 (RS): A, K3, (P1, K1) to last 2
sts, K2.
ROW 7 (WS): As row 3 (345 sts).
ROW 8 (RS): A, knit.
Bind (cast) off sts knitwise.
Rep for LH edge of the afghan.
With RS facing and using A, pick
up and knit 317 sts along bottom
edge of the afghan.
Beg with a WS row, work as folls:
ROW 1 (WS): A, inc once into the
first st, K to last 2 sts, inc once
into next st, K1 (319 sts).
ROW 2 (RS): A, knit.
ROW 3 (WS): A, inc once into the
first st, P to last 2 sts, inc once
into next st, P1. (321 sts).
ROW 4 (RS): B, K2, (yf, sl1p, yb, K1)
159 times, K1.
ROW 5 (WS): B, inc once into first
st, P1, (yfrn, P2tog) 159 times, inc
once into last st (323 sts).
ROW 6 (RS): A, K3, (P1, K1) to last 2
sts, K2.

ROW 7 (WS): As row 3 (325 sts).
ROW 8 (RS): A, knit.
Bind (cast) off sts knitwise.
Rep for top edge of afghan.
Neatly sew the border edges
together.

Order of squares

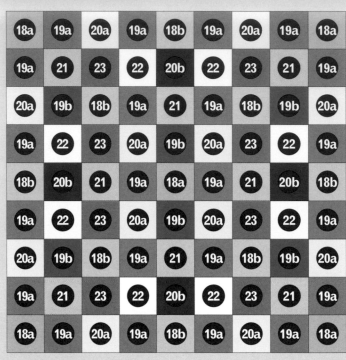

QUANTITY OF SQUARES

⑱ Mini cupcake
  ⑱ₐ First colorway   5
  ⑱♭ Second colorway   8
⑲ Icing sugar stripe
  ⑲ₐ First colorway   22
  ⑲♭ Second colorway   6
⑳ Sweetheart
  ⑳ₐ First colorway   12
  ⑳♭ Second colorway   4
㉑ Mother of pearl   8
㉒ Flocked   8
㉓ Embroidered stripe   8

⑱ Mini cupcake

SIZE

6in × 6in (15cm × 15cm)

MATERIALS

1 pair US 2–3 (3.00mm/No. 11)
  needles

⑱ₐ **First colorway** (× 5⊞ ▣)
Rowan Cotton glace
1¾oz (50g) balls
  ☐ cream (A)   ⅙
  ■ mid pink (B)   ¹/₁₂

☺ small shell buttons   24

☐ K on RS, P on WS
⊟ P on RS, K on WS

⑱♭ **Second colorway** (× 8▣)
Rowan Cotton glace
1¾oz (50g) balls
  cream (A)   ⅙
  mid pink (B)   ¹/₁₂

KNIT

Cast on 37 sts and work until
chart row 50 completed.
Bind (cast) off sts.
Using the photograph as a guide,
sew small shell buttons onto the
cream sections of 18a (first
colorway).

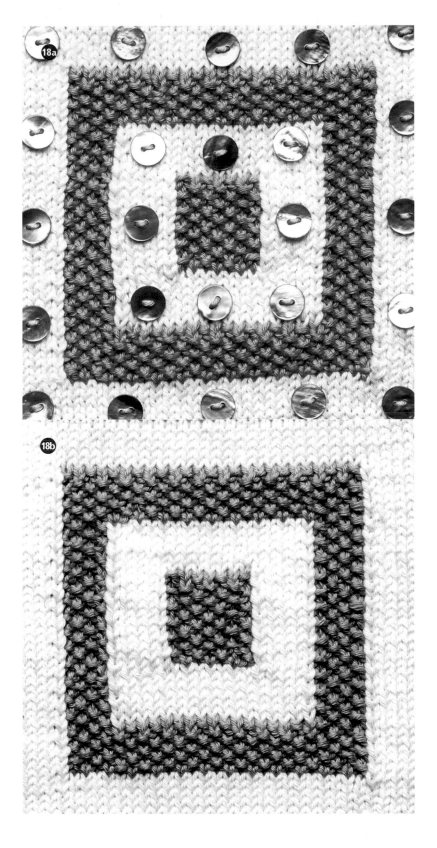

⑲ Icing sugar stripe

SIZE

6in × 6in (15cm × 15cm)

MATERIALS

1 pair US 2–3 (3.00mm/No. 11) needles

⑲ₐ First colorway (× 22◼)

Rowan Cotton Glace
1¾oz (50g) balls
mid pink (A)	¼
cream (B)	¹⁄₁₆

⑲ᵦ Second colorway (× 6◼)

Rowan Cotton Glace
1¾oz (50g) balls
purple (A)	¼
cream (B)	¹⁄₁₆

KNIT

Cast on 38 sts using A.
Note: Do not cut off yarns. Carry them up the side of the work.
ROW 1 (RS): **A, knit.**
ROW 2 (WS): **A, purl.**
ROW 3 (RS): **B, knit.**
Transfer the sts back onto the LH needle, so that the RS is facing again.
ROW 4 (RS): **A, knit.**
ROW 5 (WS): **A, purl.**
ROWS 6–7: **Rep rows 4–5.**
Transfer the sts back onto the LH needle, so that the WS is facing again.
ROW 8 (WS): **B, purl.**
ROWS 9–12: **Rep rows 1–2 twice.**
ROW 13 (RS): **As row 3.**
Transfer the sts back onto the LH needle, so that the RS is facing again.
Rep rows 4–13, 3 times more, including the transferring of sts to the LH needle.
Rep rows 4–10 once more, including the transferring of sts to the LH needle.
(50 rows)
Bind (cast) off sts.

⑳ Sweetheart

SIZE

6in × 6in (15cm × 15cm)

MATERIALS

1 pair US 2–3 (3.00mm/No. 11)
  needles

⑳ₐ First colorway (× 12 ■)

Rowan Cotton Glace
1³⁄₄oz (50g) balls
  cream   ¹⁄₃

¹⁄₈in (3mm) beads
  mauve   126

⑳ᵦ Second colorway (× 4 ■)

Rowan Cotton Glace
1³⁄₄oz (50g) balls
  purple   ¹⁄₃

¹⁄₈in (3mm) beads
  pearl   126

KNIT

Thread 126 beads onto yarn.
Cast on 37 sts.
ROW 1 (RS): Knit.
ROW 2 (WS): Purl.
ROWS 3–4: Rep rows 1–2.
ROW 5 (RS): K6, (pb, K11) twice, pb, K6.
ROW 6 (WS): Purl.
ROW 7 (RS): K5, (pb, K1, pb, K9) twice, pb, K1, pb, K5.
ROW 8 (WS): Purl.
ROW 9 (RS): K4, (pb, K3, pb, K7) twice, pb, K3, pb, K4.
ROW 10 (WS): Purl.
ROW 11 (RS): K3, (pb, K5, pb, K5) twice, pb, K5, pb, K3.
ROW 12 (WS): Purl.
ROW 13 (RS): K2, (pb, K3, pb, K3, pb, K3) twice, pb, K3, pb, K3, pb, K2.
ROW 14 (WS): P5, (pb, P1, pb, P9) twice, pb, P1, pb, P5.
ROW 15 (RS): K3, (pb, K5, pb, K5) twice, pb, K5, pb, K3.
ROW 16 (WS): Purl.
Rep rows 1–16 twice more.
Rep rows 1–2 once more.
(50 rows)
Bind (cast) off sts.

㉑ Mother of pearl

SIZE

6in × 6in (15cm × 15cm)

MATERIALS

1 pair US 2–3 (3.00mm/No. 11)
  needles

Single colorway (× 8▣)

Rowan Cotton Glace
1¾oz (50g) balls
  cream   ⅓

⅛in (3mm) beads
  silver   48

KNIT

Thread 48 silver beads onto yarn.
Cast on 38 sts.

ROW 1 (RS): K2, P1, K5, (P1, K2, P1,
K5) 3 times, P1, K2.

ROW 2 (WS): P2, K1, P5, (K1, P2,
K1, P5) 3 times, K1, P2.

ROW 3 (RS): K2, P1, (yfrn, P1,
P3tog, P1, yfrn, P1, K2, P1) 3
times, yfrn, P1, P3tog, P1, yfrn, P1,
K2.

ROW 4 (WS): P2, K2, (P3, K2, P2,
K2) 3 times, P3, K2, P2.

ROW 5 (RS): K2, P1, K2, (pb, K2,
P1, t2b, P1, K2) 3 times, pb, K2,
P1, K2.

ROW 6 (WS): P2, K1, P5, (K1, P2,
K1, P5) 3 times, K1, P2.

Rep rows 3–6, 11 times more.

(50 rows)

Bind (cast) off sts.

㉒ Flocked

SIZE

6in × 6in (15cm × 15cm)

MATERIALS

1 pair US 2–3 (3.00mm/No. 11)
  needles
Cable needle

Single colorway (× 8▣)

Rowan Cotton Glace
1¾oz (50g) balls
  cream   ⅓

KNIT

Cast on 37 sts.

ROWS 1 (RS) (INC): K1, P1, (K1, inc
once into the next st, K1, P3) 5
times, K1, inc once into the next
st, K1, P1, K1 (43 sts).

ROW 2 (WS): K2, (P1, K2, P1, K3) 5
times, P1, K2, P1, K2.

ROW 3 (RS): K1, P1, (K1, P2, K1, P3)
5 times, K1, P2, K1, P1, K1.

ROW 4 (WS): As row 2.

ROW 5 (RS): K1, P1, (t4lr, P3) 5
times, t4lr, P1, K1.

ROW 6 (WS): As row 2.

ROWS 7–10: Rep rows 3–4 twice
more.

Rep rows 5–10, 6 times more.

Rep rows 5–6 once more.

Rep row 3 once more.

NEXT ROW (WS) (DEC): K2, (P1,
K2tog, P1, K3) 5 times, P1, K2tog,
P1, K2 (37 sts).

(50 rows)

Bind (cast) off sts.

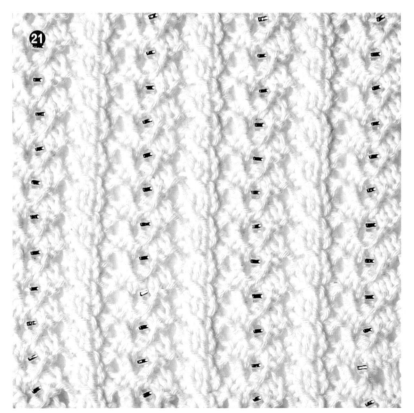

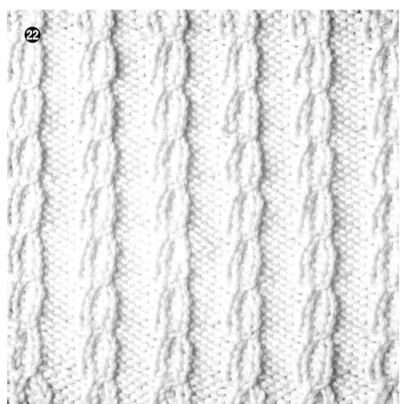

㉓ Embroidered stripe

SIZE

6in × 6in (15cm × 15cm)

MATERIALS

1 pair US 2–3 (3.00mm/No. 11)
  needles

Single colorway (x 8■)
Rowan Cotton Glace
1¾oz (50g) balls
  lilac   ⅕
  cream   ⅟₁₆

KNIT

Cast on 37 sts.
ROW 1 (RS): **A, knit.**
ROW 2 (WS): **A, purl.**
ROWS 3–4: **Rep rows 1–2.**
ROW 5 (RS): **K2B, (yf, sl1p, yb, K1B) 17 times, K1B.**
ROW 6 (WS): **P2B, (yon, P2togB) 17 times, P1B.**
ROW 7 (RS): **K2A, (P1A, K1A) 17 times, K1A.**
ROW 8 (WS): **A, purl.**
ROWS 9–10: **Rep rows 1–2.**
Rep rows 1–10, 4 times more.
(50 rows)
Bind (cast) off sts.

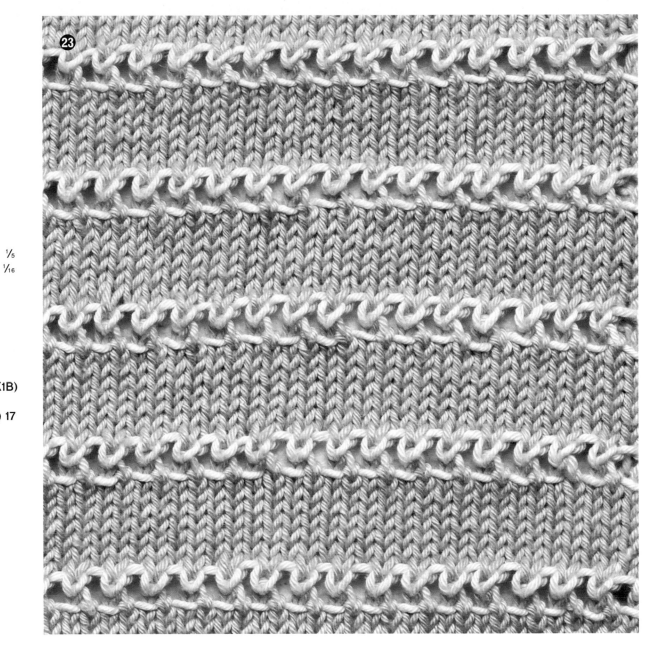

fish

Cool, sparkling streams, the flash of a darting fish on a summer's afternoon, and ripples of running water are all captured in this design. Crisp cottons in cool shades of blue and green are mixed with touches of soft lilac, purple, and yellow to create a colorful afghan. Sequins simulate fish scales and small silver and blue beads represent ripples in a trickling stream. A pattern combining cables and bobbles suggests water plants moving gently in the current.

SIZE
54in × 42in (135cm × 105cm)

MATERIALS
1 pair US 2–3 (3.00mm/No. 11)
needles
1 pair US 2 (2.75mm/No. 12)
needles
2 circular US 2 (2.75mm/No. 12)
needles 32in (80cm) length
Cable needle

Yarn
Rowan Cotton Glace
1¾oz (50g) balls

purple	4
pink	4
yellow	3
mid green	6
light turquoise	6
cream	1
lilac	2
dark green	2

Beads
⅛in (3mm) beads

blue	1277
silver	1277
pale pink	17

Sequins
5/16 (8mm) sequins

light turquoise	918

Quantities given for individual
squares are approximate fractions
of a ball.

GAUGE (TENSION)
25 sts and 34 rows to 4in (10cm)
measured over stockinette
(stocking) stitch using US 2
(3.00mm/No. 11) needles.

ABBREVIATIONS
See page 127.

FINISHING
The sizes given for the finished
afghan and individual squares are
approximate. The number of
stitches in a row, and the number
of rows in a square differ in some
instances. Therefore, when sewing
pieces together, ease the extra
stitches or rows into the adjoining
square.

   Press the individual squares
using a damp cloth and a warm
iron. Sew the squares together,
joining bound (cast) off edge of
one square to the cast-on edge of
the next square, easing in stitches,
if necessary, to form vertical
strips. Sew the vertical strips
together, easing in rows, if
necessary, to create one block.

Edging

MATERIALS
2 circular US 2 (2.75mm/No. 12)
needles 32in (80cm) length

Yarn
Rowan Cotton Glace
1¾oz (50g) balls

dark green (A)	½
mid green (B)	1

KNIT
With RS facing and using A, pick
up and knit 326 sts along the RH
edge of the afghan.
Beg with a WS row, work as folls:
ROW 1 (WS): Using A, inc once into
first st, K to last 2 sts, inc once
into next st, K1 (328 sts).
ROW 2 (RS): A, purl.
Push sts to other end of circular
needle so that the RS is facing
again.
ROW 3 (RS): Using B, inc once into
first st, K to last 2 sts, inc once
into next st, K1 (330 sts).
ROW 4 (WS): B, knit.
ROW 5 (RS): Using B, inc once into
first st, P to last 2 sts, inc once

into next st, K1 (332 sts).
Push sts to other end of circular
needle so that the RS is facing
again.
Using B, bind (cast) off sts
knitwise.
Rep for LH edge of the afghan.
With RS facing and A, pick up and
knit 251 sts along bottom edge of
the afghan.
Rep edging as for RH and LH
edges.
Rep for top edge of afghan.
Neatly sew border edges together.

Order of squares

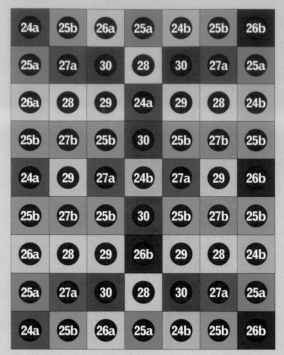

QUANTITY OF SQUARES

㉔ Fishes 1
- ㉔ₐ First colorway — 4
- ㉔ᵦ Second colorway — 5

㉕ Ripple
- ㉕ₐ First colorway — 6
- ㉕ᵦ Second colorway — 12

㉖ Fishes 2
- ㉖ₐ First colorway — 4
- ㉖ᵦ Second colorway — 4

㉗ Bright stripe
- ㉗ₐ First colorway — 6
- ㉗ᵦ Second colorway — 4

㉘ Sun, sea and surf — 6

㉙ Fish scales — 6

㉚ Seaweed — 6

㉔ Fishes 1

SIZE
6in × 6in (15cm × 15cm)

MATERIALS
1 pair US 2–3 (3.00mm/No. 11) needles

㉔ₐ First colorway (× 4⊞ ▣)
Rowan Cotton Glace
1¾oz (50g) balls
- ■ purple (A) — ⅕
- ■ pink (B) — ¹⁄₁₂
- □ yellow (C) — ¹⁄₁₂
- ■ mid green (D) — ¹⁄₁₂

⅛in (3mm) beads
- ◌ silver — 1
- ◌ blue — 1
- ◌ pale pink — 1

□ K on RS, P on WS
⊟ P on RS, K on WS

㉔ᵦ Second colorway (× 5▣)
Rowan Cotton Glace
1¾oz (50g) balls
- pink (A) — ⅕
- light turquoise (B) — ¹⁄₁₂
- yellow (C) — ¹⁄₁₂
- purple (D) — ¹⁄₁₂

⅛in (3mm) beads
- pale pink — 1
- blue — 1
- silver — 1

KNIT
Thread beads onto yarns when needed.
Cast on 38 sts using A and work until chart row 49 completed.
Bind (cast) off sts.

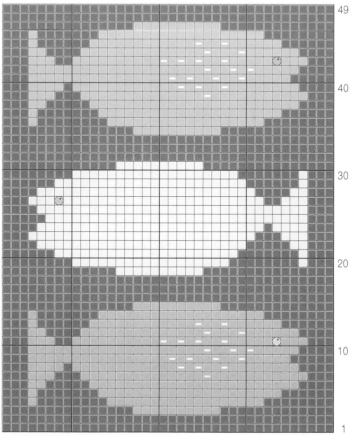

㉕ Ripple

SIZE
6in × 6in (15cm × 15cm)

MATERIALS
1 pair US 2–3 (3.00mm/No. 11)
  needles

㉕ⓐ First colorway (× 6⊞ ▣)
Rowan Cotton Glace
1³⁄₄oz (50g) balls
☐ mid green   ¹⁄₄

¹⁄₈in (3mm) beads
◌ silver   70
◍ blue   70

☐ K on RS, P on WS

㉕ⓑ Second colorway (× 12▣)
Rowan Cotton Glace
1³⁄₄oz (50g) balls
  light turquoise   ¹⁄₄

¹⁄₈in (3mm) beads
  silver   70
  blue   70

KNIT
Thread beads onto yarn in the foll
sequence: 1 silver, 1 blue, 1 silver,
1 blue, 1 silver, 1 blue, 1 silver,
2 blue, 1 silver, 1 blue, 2 silver,
1 blue, 1 silver, 2 blue, 1 silver,
1 blue, 1 silver, 1 blue, 1 silver, 1
blue, 1 silver, 1 blue, 1 silver, 1 blue,
2 silver, 1 blue, 1 silver, 2 blue,
1 silver, 1 blue, 2 silver, 1 blue,
1 silver, 1 blue, (1 silver, 1 blue,

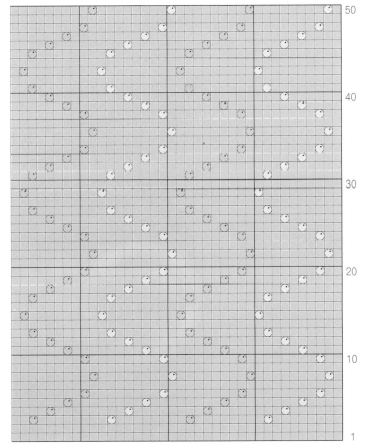

1 silver, 1 blue, 1 silver, 1 blue,
1 silver, 2 blue, 1 silver, 1 blue,
2 silver, 1 blue, 1 silver, 2 blue,
1 silver, 1 blue, 1 silver, 1 blue,
1 silver, 1 blue, 1 silver, 1 blue,
1 silver, 1 blue, 2 silver, 1 blue,
1 silver, 2 blue, 1 silver, 1 blue,
2 silver, 1 blue, 1 silver, 1 blue)
twice, 1 silver, 1 blue, 1 silver,
1 blue, 1 silver, 1 blue, 1 silver,
2 blue, 1 silver, 1 blue, 2 silver,
1 blue, 1 silver, 2 blue, 1 silver,
1 blue, 1 silver.

Cast on 38 sts and work until
chart row 50 completed.
Bind (cast) off sts.

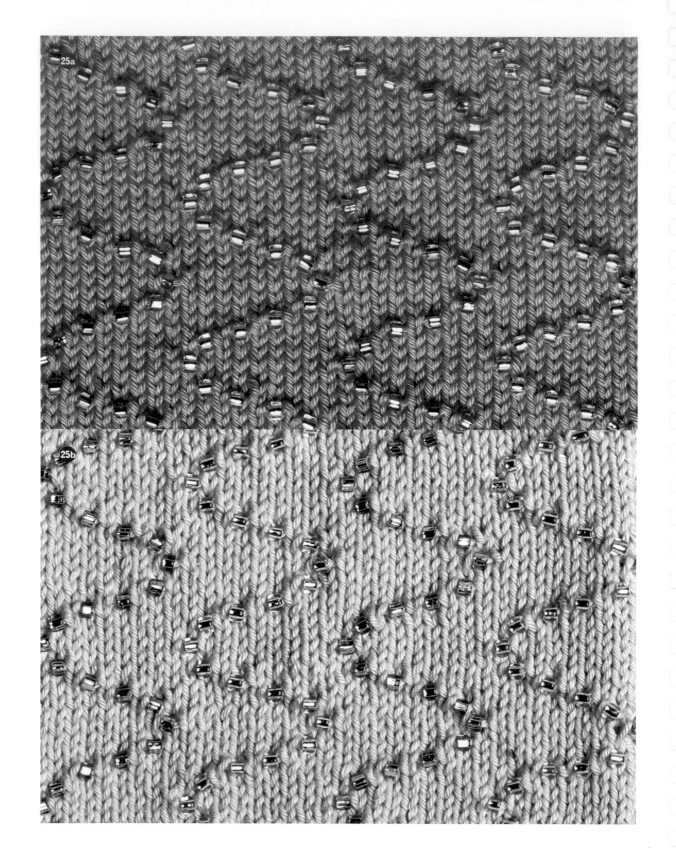

㉖ Fishes 2

SIZE

6in × 6in (15cm × 15cm)

MATERIALS

1 pair US 2–3 (3.00mm/No. 11)
  needles

㉖ₐ First colorway (× 4⊞ ■)

Rowan Cotton Glace
1¾oz (50g) balls

▨	pink (A)	⅕
■	purple (B)	1/12
☐	yellow (C)	1/12
▨	light turquoise (D)	1/12

⅛in (3mm) beads

⦾	silver	1
⦿	blue	1
⦿	pale pink	1

☐ K on RS, P on WS
⊟ P on RS, K on WS

㉖ᵦ Second colorway (× 4■)

Rowan Cotton Glace
1¾oz (50g) balls

purple (A)	⅕
mid green (B)	1/12
yellow (C)	1/12
pink (D)	1/12

⅛in (3mm) beads

pale pink	1
blue	1
silver	1

KNIT

Thread beads onto yarns when
needed.
Cast on 38 sts using A and work
until chart row 49 completed.
Bind (cast) off sts.

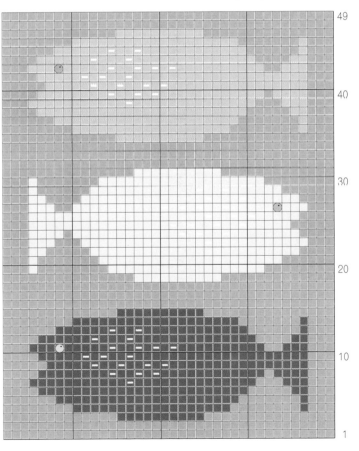

㉗ Bright stripe

SIZE

6in × 6in (15cm × 15cm)

MATERIALS

1 pair US 2–3 (3.00mm/No. 11)
    needles
1 pair US 2 (2.75mm/No. 12)
    needles

㉗ₐ First colorway (× 6■)

Rowan Cotton Glace
1¾oz (50g) balls

purple (A)	¼
yellow (B)	¹⁄₂₅
light turquoise (C)	¹⁄₁₂

㉗ᵦ Second colorway (× 4■)

Rowan Cotton Glace
1¾oz (50g) balls

pink (A)	¼
yellow (B)	¹⁄₂₅
light turquoise (C)	¹⁄₁₂

KNIT

Cast on 38 sts using A and US
2–3 (3.00mm/No. 11) needles.
ROW 1 (RS): **A, knit.**
ROW 2 (WS): **A, purl.**
ROW 3 (RS): **A, knit.**
Change to US 2 (2.75mm/No. 12)
needles.
ROW 4 (WS): **B, purl.**
ROW 5 (RS): **B, purl.**
Change to US 2–3 (3.00mm/No.
11) needles.
ROW 6 (WS): **A, purl.**
ROWS 7–8: **Rep rows 1–2.**
ROW 9 (RS): **C, knit.**
ROW 10 (WS): **C, purl.**
ROW 11 (RS): **C, knit.**
ROW 12 (WS): **A, purl.**
ROWS 13–14: **Rep rows 1–2.**
Change to US 2 (2.75mm/No. 12)
needles.
ROW 15 (RS): **B, knit.**
ROW 16 (WS): **B, knit.**
Change to US 2–3 (3.00mm/No.
11) needles.
ROWS 17–18: **Rep rows 1–2.**
ROW 19 (RS): **A, knit.**
ROW 20 (WS): **C, purl.**
ROWS 21–22: **Rep rows 9–10.**
Rep rows 1–22 once more.
Rep rows 1–8 once more.
(52 rows)
Bind (cast) off sts.

㉘ Sun, sea and surf

SIZE
6in × 6in (15cm × 15cm)

MATERIALS
1 pair US 2–3 (3.00mm/No. 11)
   needles

Single colorway (× 6■)
Rowan Cotton Glace
1¾oz (50g) balls
   light turquoise (A)   ⅕
   cream (B)   ¹⁄₁₀
   yellow (C)   ¹⁄₁₆

KNIT
Cast on 38 sts using A.
ROWS 1 (RS): A, knit.
ROW 2 (WS): A, purl.
ROW 3 (RS): K2B, (P2B, K2B) 9 times.
ROW 4 (WS): P2C, (K2C, P2C) 9 times.
ROW 5 (RS): A, knit.
ROW 6 (WS): K2A, (P2A, K2A) 9 times.
ROW 7 (RS): P2A, (K2A, P2A) 9 times.
ROW 8 (WS): P2B, (K2B, P2B) 9 times.
ROW 9 (RS): K2C, (P2C, K2C) 9 times.
ROW 10 (WS): A, purl.
ROW 11 (RS): P2A, (K2A, P2A) 9 times.
ROW 12 (WS): K2A, (P2A, K2A) 9 times.
Rep rows 3–12, 3 times more.
Rep rows 3–10 once more.
(50 rows)
Bind (cast) off sts.

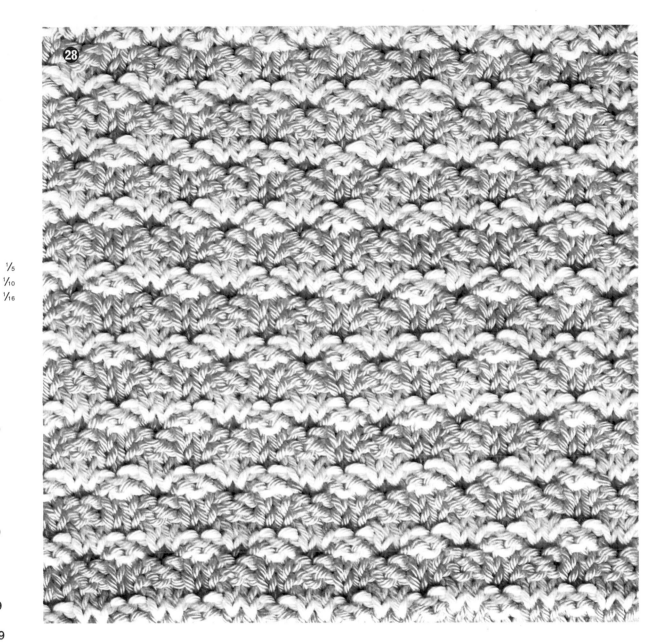

㉙ Fish scales

SIZE
6in × 6in (15cm × 15cm)

MATERIALS
1 pair US 2–3 (3.00mm/No. 11)
 needles

Single colorway (× 6■)
Rowan Cotton Glace
1¾oz (50g) balls
 lilac   ⅓

Sequins
⅝in (8mm) sequins
 light turquoise   153

KNIT
Note: When placing sequins, smooth them down so they lie flat on the work and are all facing the same way.
Thread 153 sequins onto yarn.
Cast on 38 sts.
ROW 1 (RS): Knit.
ROW 2 (WS): Purl.
ROW 3 (RS): Knit.
ROW 4 (WS): Purl.
ROW 5 (RS): K3, (ps, K1) 17 times, K1.
ROW 6 (WS): Purl.
ROW 7 (RS): (K1, P1) 19 times.
ROW 8 (WS): Purl.
ROW 9 (RS): Knit.
ROW 10 (WS): Purl.
Rep rows 5–10, 7 times more.
Rep rows 5–6 once more.
(54 rows)
Bind (cast) off sts.

㉚ Seaweed

SIZE

6in × 6in (15cm × 15cm)

MATERIALS

1 pair US 2–3 (3.00mm/No. 11)
  needles
Cable needle

Single colorway (× 6■)

Rowan Cotton Glace
1¾oz (50g) balls
  mid green (A)   ½
  dark green (B)   ⅕

KNIT

Note: Yarn B is introduced into the work 1 row before the bobble is made. Cut B into short lengths of approximately 12in (30cm) and join in when required.

Cast on 38 sts using A.

ROW 1 (RS) (INC): **P3A, (K1A, using A inc once into next st, K1A, using A inc once into next st, P3A) 5 times (48 sts).**

ROW 2 (WS): **K3A, (P6A, K3A) 5 times.**

ROW 3 (RS): **P3A, (K6A, P3A) 5 times.**

ROW 4 (WS): **As row 2.**

ROWS 5–6: **Rep rows 3–4.**

ROW 7 (RS): **P3A, (c6fA, P3A) 5 times.**

ROWS 8–9: **Rep rows 2–3.**

ROW 10 (WS): **K3A, (P4A, P1B, P1A, K3A) 5 times.**

ROW 11 (RS): **P3A, (K1A, mbB, K4A, P3A) 5 times.**

ROW 12 (WS): **As row 2.**

ROWS 13–16: **Rep rows 3–4 twice.**

ROW 17 (RS): **P3A, (c6bA, P3A) 5 times.**

ROWS 18–19: **Rep rows 2–3.**

ROW 20 (WS): **K3A, (P1A, P1B, P4A, K3A) 5 times.**

ROW 21 (RS): **P3A, (K4A, mbB, K1A, P3A) 5 times.**

ROW 22 (WS): **As row 2.**

Rep rows 3–22 once more.

Rep rows 3–8 once more.

Rep rows 3–4 once more.

NEXT ROW (RS) (DEC): **P3A, [K1A, (K2togA) twice, K1A, P3A] 5 times (38 sts).**

(51 rows)

Bind (cast) off sts.

floor coverings

This is a one color design using texture to simulate floor coverings found in the home. There is a variety of finishes to draw upon—sisal, wood, rush matting, and rubber, for example – and the challenge was to meld these textures into one unified design. Floor coverings offers an opportunity to any beginner to try a variety of stitch textures, such as cable, basketweave, slip stitch patterns, and variations on seed stitch. In the example shown, I have chosen to use icewater blue, a neutral, steely shade, but the knitter can choose a shade to match existing home furnishings.

SIZE
88in × 61in (220cm × 153cm)

ABBREVIATIONS
See page 127.

MATERIALS
1 pair US 5 (3.75mm/No. 9)
   needles
2 circular US 2–3 (3.00mm/No. 11)
   needles 32in (80cm) length
Cable needle

Yarn
Rowan Handknit DK Cotton
1¾oz (50g) balls
   mid blue   62

Quantities given for individual squares are approximate fractions of a ball.

Beads
³⁄₁₆oz in (5mm) beads
   silver   162

GAUGE (TENSION)
22 sts and 30 rows to 4in (10cm) measured over stockinette (stocking) stitch using US 5 (3.75mm/No. 9) needles.

FINISHING
The sizes given for the finished afghan and individual squares are approximate. The number of stitches in a row, and the number of rows in a square differ in some instances. Therefore, when sewing pieces together, ease the extra stitches or rows into the adjoining square.

   Press the individual squares using a damp cloth and a warm iron. Sew the squares together, joining bound- (cast-) off edge of one square to the cast-on edge of the next square, easing in stitches, if necessary, to form vertical strips. Sew the vertical strips together, easing in rows, if necessary, to create one block.

Edging

MATERIALS

2 circular US 2–3 (3.00mm/No. 11) needles 32in (80cm) length

Yarn

Rowan Handknit DK Cotton
1¾oz (50g) balls
    mid blue   4⅛

KNIT

With RS facing, pick up and knit 492 sts along the RH edge of the afghan.

Beg with a WS row, cont to work in double seed (moss) stitch as folls:

ROW 1 (WS): (K2, P2) to end of row.

ROW 2 (RS): Inc once into first st, K1, (P2, K2) to last 2 sts, inc once into next st, K1 (494 sts).

ROW 3 (WS): K1, (P2, K2) to last st, P1.

ROW 4 (RS): Inc once into first st, (P2, K2) to last 5 sts, P2, K1, inc once into next st, P1 (496 sts).

Keeping the double seed (moss) stitch patt correct, work 6 more rows, inc 1 st at each end of RS rows, taking extra sts into the patt (502 sts).

Bind (cast) off sts knitwise.

Rep for LH edge of afghan.

With RS facing, pick up and knit 328 sts along bottom edge of the afghan.

Rep edging as for RH and LH edges.

Rep for top edge of afghan.

Neatly sew border edges together.

Order of squares

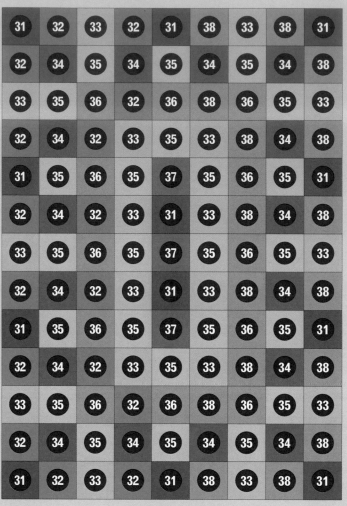

QUANTITY OF SQUARES

③¹ Ribbed cable		12
³² Sisal		16
³³ Rubber mat		18
³⁴ Cord		16
³⁵ Doormat		24
³⁶ Wood grain		12
³⁷ Grid		3
³⁸ Sisal II		16

③¹ Ribbed cable

SIZE

6¾in × 6¾in (17cm × 17cm)

MATERIALS

1 pair US 5 (3.75mm/No. 9) needles
Cable needle

Single colorway (× 12■)

Rowan Handknit DK Cotton
1¾oz (50g) balls
    mid blue   ⁷⁄₁₀

KNIT

Cast on 37 sts.

ROW 1 (RS) (INC): P2, (inc once in each of next 5 sts, P2) 5 times (62 sts).

ROW 2 (WS): K2, [(P1, K1) twice, P2, (K1, P1) twice, K2] 5 times.

ROW 3 (RS): P2, [(K1, P1) twice, K2, (P1, K1) twice, P2] 5 times.

ROWS 4–7: Rep rows 2–3 twice.

ROW 8 (WS): As row 2.

ROW 9 (RS): P2, [sl next 5 sts onto cable needle and hold at back of work, (K1, P1) twice, K1, then (K1, P1) twice, K1 from the cable needle, P2, sl next 5 sts onto cable needle and hold at front of work, (K1, P1) twice, K1, then (K1, P1) twice, K1 from the cable needle, P2] twice, sl next 5 sts onto cable needle and hold at back of work, (K1, P1) twice, K1, then (K1, P1) twice, K1 from the cable needle, P2.

ROWS 10–19: Rep rows 2–3, 5 times.

ROW 20 (WS): **As row 2.**
ROW 21 (RS): **As row 9.**
ROWS 22–31: **Rep rows 2–3,**
5 times.
ROW 32 (WS): **As row 2.**
ROW 33 (RS): **As row 9.**
ROWS 34–43: **Rep rows 2–3,**
5 times.
ROW 44 (WS): **As row 2.**
ROW 45 (RS): **As row 9.**
ROWS 46–49: **Rep rows 2–3 twice.**
ROW 50 (WS) (DEC): **K2, [(P2tog) 5**
times, K2] 5 times (37 sts).
Bind (cast) off sts.

㉜ Sisal

SIZE
6¾in × 6¾in (17cm × 17cm)

MATERIALS
1 pair US 5 (3.75mm/No. 9)
  needles

Single colorway (× 16■)
Rowan Handknit DK Cotton
1¾oz (50g) balls
  mid blue   ½

KNIT
Cast on 37 sts.
ROW 1 (RS): **K1, (P2, K1) 12 times.**
ROW 2 (WS): **K3, (P1, K2) 11 times,**
K1.
ROW 3 (RS): **K1, P1, (K1, P2) 11**
times, K2.
ROW 4 (WS): **K1, (P1, K2) 12 times.**
ROW 5 (RS): **K2, (P2, K1) 11 times,**
P1, K1.
ROW 6 (WS): **K2, (P1, K2) 11 times,**
P1, K1.
Rep rows 1–6, 7 times more.
Rep rows 1–2 once more.
(50 rows)
Bind (cast) off sts.

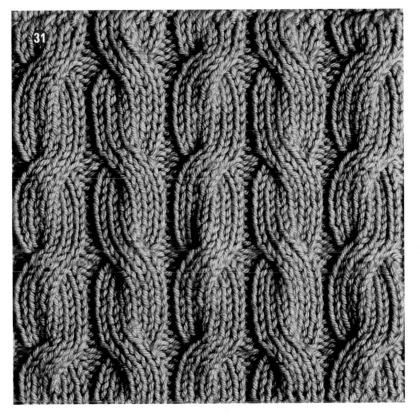

㉝ Rubber mat

SIZE
6¾in × 6¾in (17cm × 17cm)

MATERIALS
1 pair US 5 (3.75mm/No. 9)
  needles

Single colorway (× 18⊞ ▣)
Rowan Handknit DK Cotton
1¾oz (50g) balls
▢ mid blue   ½

³⁄₁₆in (5mm) beads
⊙ silver   9

☐ K on RS, P on WS
⊟ P on RS, K on WS

Note: Work chart row 10 (WS) as
folls: (K2, P4, yb, sl bead up yarn
to front of work, sl 2 sts purlwise,
yf leaving bead in front of slipped
sts, P4) 3 times, K2.

KNIT
Thread 9 silver beads onto yarn.
Cast on 38 sts.
Beg with a RS row, work chart
rows 1–16, 3 times.
Rep chart rows 1–2 once more.
(50 rows)
Bind (cast) off sts.

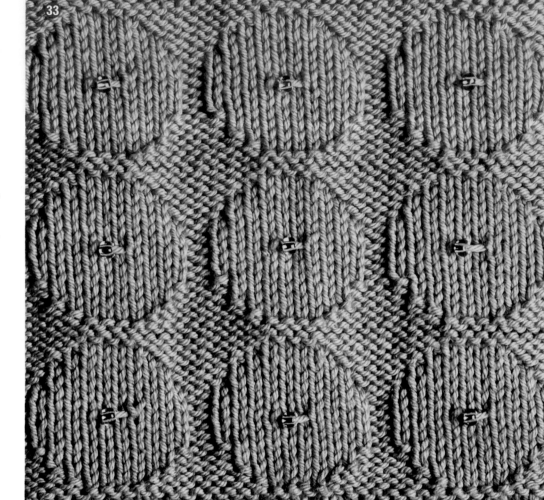

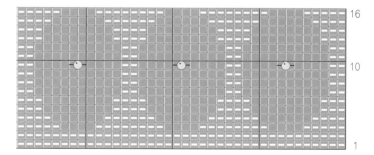

㉞ Cord

SIZE
6¾in × 6¾in (17cm × 17cm)

MATERIALS
1 pair US 5 (3.75mm/No. 9)
   needles
cable needle

Single colorway (× 16■)
Rowan Handknit DK Cotton
1¾oz (50g) balls
   mid blue   ½

KNIT
Cast on 38 sts.
ROW 1 (RS): K1, P1, (K2, P2) 8
times, K2, P1, K1.
ROW 2 (WS): K2, (P2, K2) 9 times.
ROW 3 (RS): K1, P1, (t2f, P2, K2,
P2) 4 times, t2f, P1, K1.
ROW 4 (WS): As row 2.
ROW 5 (RS): K1, P1, (K2, P2, t2f,
P2) 4 times, K2, P1, K1.
ROW 6 (WS): As row 2.
Rep rows 3–6, 11 times more.
(50 rows)
Bind (cast) off sts.

㉟ Doormat

SIZE
6¾in × 6¾in (17cm × 17cm)

MATERIALS
1 pair US 5 (3.75mm/No. 9)
   needles

Single colorway (× 24■)
Rowan Handknit DK Cotton
1¾oz (50g) balls
   mid blue   ½

KNIT
Cast on 37 sts.
ROW 1 (RS): K1, (P1, K1) 18 times.
ROW 2 (WS): K2, (P1, K1) 17 times,
K1.
ROW 3 (RS): As row 1.
ROW 4 (WS): K1, (P1, K1) 18 times.
ROW 5 (RS): K2, (P1, K1) 17 times,
K1.
ROW 6 (WS): As row 4.
Rep rows 1–6, 7 times more.
Rep row 1 once more.
(49 rows)
Bind (cast) off sts.

36 Wood grain

SIZE

6¾in × 6¾in (17cm × 17cm)

MATERIALS

1 pair US 5 (3.75mm/No. 9)
   needles

Single colorway (× 12⊞ ▣)
Rowan Handknit DK Cotton
1¾oz (50g) balls
   ▣ mid blue   ½

☐ K on RS, P on WS
⊟ P on RS, K on WS

KNIT

Cast on 38 sts and work until
chart row 50 completed.
Bind (cast) off sts.

37 Grid

SIZE

6¾in × 6¾in (17cm × 17cm)

MATERIALS

1 pair US 5 (3.75mm/No. 9)
   needles

Single colorway (× 3▣)
Rowan Handknit DK Cotton
1¾oz (50g) balls
   mid blue   ½

KNIT

Cast on 37 sts.
ROW 1 (RS): P9, (K1, P8) 3 times,
P1.
ROW 2 (WS): K9, (P1, K8) 3 times,
K1.
ROW 3 (RS): P9, (yb, sl1p, yf, P8)
3 times, P1.
ROWS 4–11: Rep rows 2–3,
4 times.
ROW 12 (WS): Purl.
ROW 13 (RS): K9, (sl1p, K8)
3 times, K1.
ROWS 14–23: Rep rows 2–3,
5 times.
ROW 24 (WS): As row 2.
ROW 25 (RS): K9, (sl1p, K8) 3 times,
K1.
ROW 26 (WS): Purl.
ROW 27 (RS): As row 3.
ROWS 28–50: Rep rows 2–24
once more.
Bind (cast) off sts.

38 Sisal II

SIZE

6¾in × 6¾in (17cm × 17cm)

MATERIALS

1 pair US 5 (3.75mm/No. 9)
   needles

Single colorway (× 16▣)
Rowan Handknit DK Cotton
1¾oz (50g) balls
   mid blue   ½

KNIT

Cast on 37 sts.
ROW 1 (RS): K1, (P2, K1) 12 times.
ROW 2 (WS): K3, (P1, K2) 11 times,
K1.
ROW 3 (RS): K2, (P2, K1) 11 times,
P1, K1.
ROW 4 (WS): K2, (P1, K2) 11 times,
P1, K1.
ROW 5 (RS): K1, P1, (K1, P2) 11
times, K2.
ROW 6 (WS): K1, (P1, K2) 12 times.
Rep rows 1–6, 7 times more.
Rep rows 1–2 once more.
(50 rows).
Bind (cast) off sts.

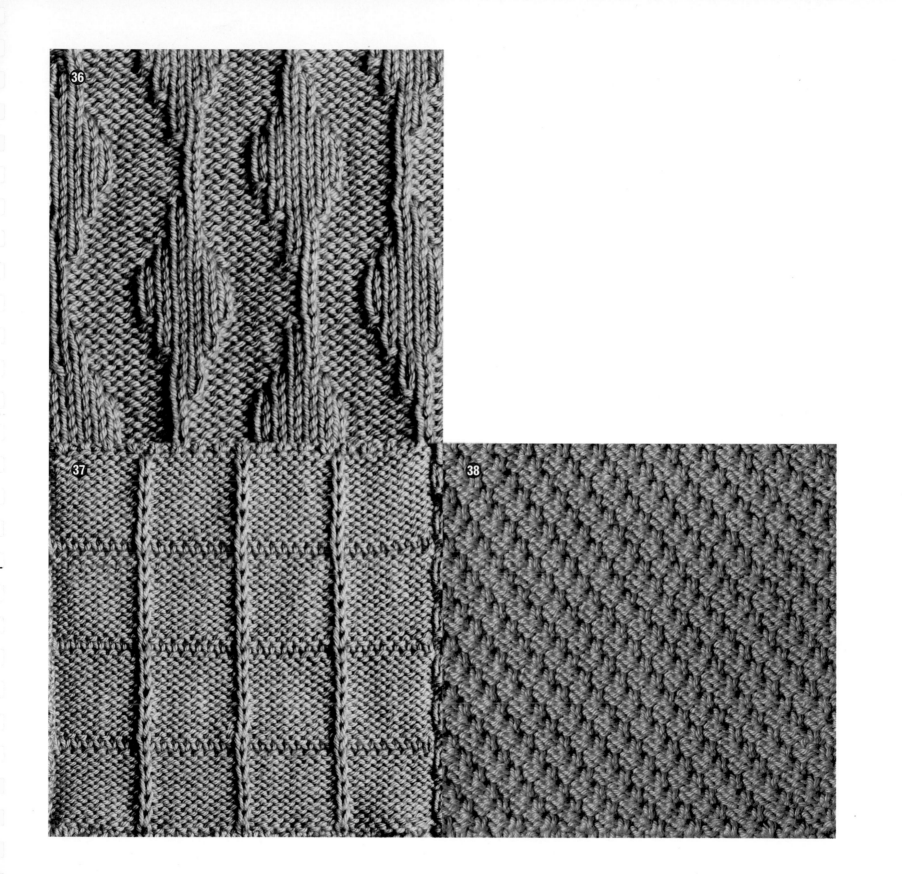

fruity

This is a fun afghan based on simplified shapes of various fruits chosen specifically for their attractive colors and design possibilities. The details, such as seeds and markings on the skin of fruits, are depicted using beads, Swiss-darning, and seed stitches, adding to the overall decorative effect. The fruit shapes alternate with bright stripes using colors from the fruit squares. The linking color for the design is green, representing peel, worked in an overall knit and purl stitch pattern to simulate the textured skin of fruit.

SIZE
77in × 77in (193cm × 193cm)

MATERIALS
1 pair US 9 (5.5mm/No. 5) needles
2 circular US 8 (5.00mm/No. 6)
  needles
Cable needle

Yarn
Rowan Cotton Rope
1¾oz (50g) balls
purple	10
yellow	12
white	21
pink	6
green	24
blue	10
orange	10

Rowan Cotton Glace
1¾oz (50g) balls
dark green	1

(used double throughout)

Beads
³⁄₁₆in (5mm) beads
white	60
black	230

Quantities given for individual squares are approximate fractions of a ball.

GAUGE (TENSION)
16 sts and 24 rows to 4in (10cm) measured over stockinette (stocking) stitch using US 9 (5.5mm/No. 5) needles.

NOTE
Single stitch outlines on squares ㉟, ㊶, ㊷, ㊸ and ㊹ can be Swiss-darned after knitting (see page 122).

ABBREVIATIONS
See page 127.

FINISHING
The sizes given for the finished afghan and individual squares are approximate. The number of stitches in a row, and the number of rows in a square differ in some instances. Therefore, when sewing pieces together, ease the extra stitches or rows into the adjoining square.

Press the individual squares using a damp cloth and a warm iron. Sew the squares together, joining bound- (cast-) off edge of one square to the cast-on edge of the next square, easing in stitches, if necessary, to form vertical strips. Sew the vertical strips together, easing in rows, if necessary, to create one block.

Edging

MATERIALS
2 circular US 8 (5.00mm/No. 6) needles

Yarn
Rowan Cotton Rope
1¾oz (50g) balls
purple (A)	5
yellow (B)	1
pink (C)	2

KNIT
With RS facing and using A, pick up and knit 335 sts along the RH edge of the afghan.
Beg with a WS row, cont to work as folls:
ROW 1 (WS): Using A, inc once into first st, P to last 2 sts, inc once into next st, P1 (337 sts).
ROW 2 (RS): B, purl.
ROW 3 (WS): Using A, inc once into first st, K to last 2 sts, inc once into next st, K1 (339 sts).
ROW 4 (RS): A, knit.
ROWS 5-6: Rep rows 3–4.
ROW 7 (WS): As row 3.
Push sts to other end of circular needle so that the WS is facing again.
ROW 8 (WS): B, knit.
ROW 9 (RS): Using A, inc once into first st, P to last 2 sts, inc once into next st, P1 (345 sts).
ROW 10 (WS): C, purl.
ROW 11 (RS): Using C, inc once into first st, P to last 2 sts, inc once into next st, P1 (347 sts).
Using C, bind (cast) off sts knitwise.
Rep for LH edge of afghan.
With RS facing and A, pick up and knit 319 sts along bottom edge of the afghan.
Rep edging as for RH and LH edges.
Rep for top edge of afghan.
Neatly sew border edges together.

Order of squares

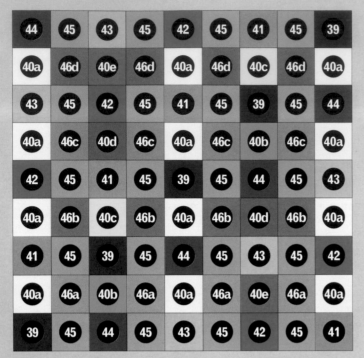

QUANTITY OF SQUARES

㊴ Lemon		5
㊵ Fruity cable		
	㊵ₐ First colorway	12
	㊵ᵦ Second colorway	2
	㊵ᵧ Third colorway	2
	㊵ₐ Fourth colorway	2
	㊵ₑ Fifth colorway	2
㊶ Apple		5
㊷ Orange		5
㊸ Melon		5
㊹ Kiwi		5
㊺ Peel		20
㊻ Fruity stripe		
	㊻ₐ First colorway	4
	㊻ᵦ Second colorway	4
	㊻ᵧ Third colorway	4
	㊻ₐ Fourth colorway	4

㊴ Lemon

SIZE
8½in × 8½in (22cm × 22cm)

MATERIALS
1 pair US 9 (5.5mm/No. 5) needles

Single colorway (× 5⊞ ▣)
Rowan Cotton Rope
1¾oz (50g) balls

■	purple (A)	³/₅
☐	yellow (B)	¼
☐	white (C)	¼

³/₁₆in (5mm) beads
⊙ white   6

☐ K on RS, P on WS
⊟ P on RS, K on WS

KNIT
Thread 6 white beads onto B.
Cast on 37 sts and work until
chart row 50 completed.
Bind (cast) off sts.

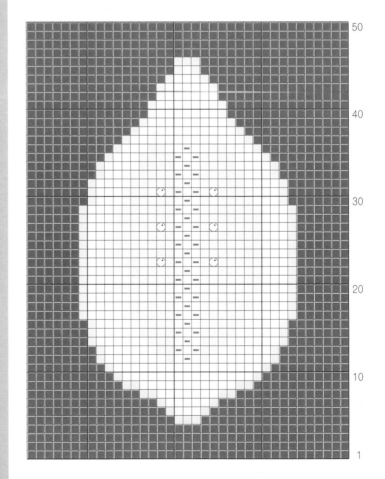

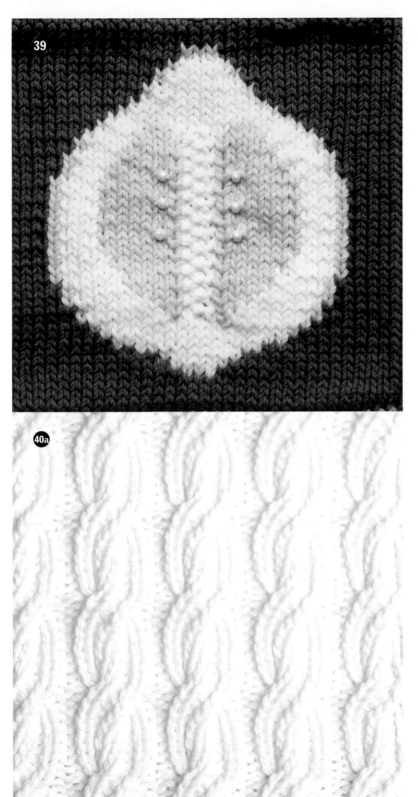

39

40a

⓺ Fruity cable

SIZE

8½in × 8½in (22cm × 22cm)

MATERIALS

1 pair US 9 (5.5mm/No. 5) needles
Cable needle

⓪ₐ First colorway (× 12◼)
Rowan Cotton Rope
1¾oz (50g) balls
white   1⅓

⓪ᵦ Second colorway (× 2◼)
Rowan Cotton Rope
1¾oz (50g) balls
blue   1⅓

⓪ᵪ Third colorway (× 2◼)
Rowan Cotton Rope
1¾oz (50g) balls
yellow   1⅓

⓪ₔ Fourth colorway (× 2◼)
Rowan Cotton Rope
1¾oz (50g) balls
purple   1⅓

⓪ₑ Fifth colorway (× 2◼)
Rowan Cotton Rope
1¾oz 50g) balls
orange   1⅓

KNIT

Cast on 37 sts.
ROW 1 (RS) (INC): **P2, (K1, inc once into each of next 3 sts, K1, P2) 5 times (52 sts).**
ROW 2 (WS): **K2, (P1, K2, P2, K2, P1, K2) 5 times.**
ROW 3 (RS): **P2, (K1, P2, K2, P2, K1, P2) 5 times.**
ROW 4 (WS): **As row 2.**
ROWS 5–6: **Rep rows 3–4.**
ROW 7 (RS): **P2, (sl next 4 sts onto cable needle and hold at back of work, K1, P2, K1, then K1, P2, K1 from cable needle, P2) 5 times.**
ROW 8 (WS): **As row 2.**
ROWS 9–16: **Rep rows 3–4, 4 times.**
Rep rows 7–16, 3 times more.
Rep rows 7–10 once more.
NEXT ROW (RS) (DEC): **P2, [K1, (K2tog) 3 times, K1, P2] 5 times (37 sts).**
(51 rows)
Bind (cast) off sts.

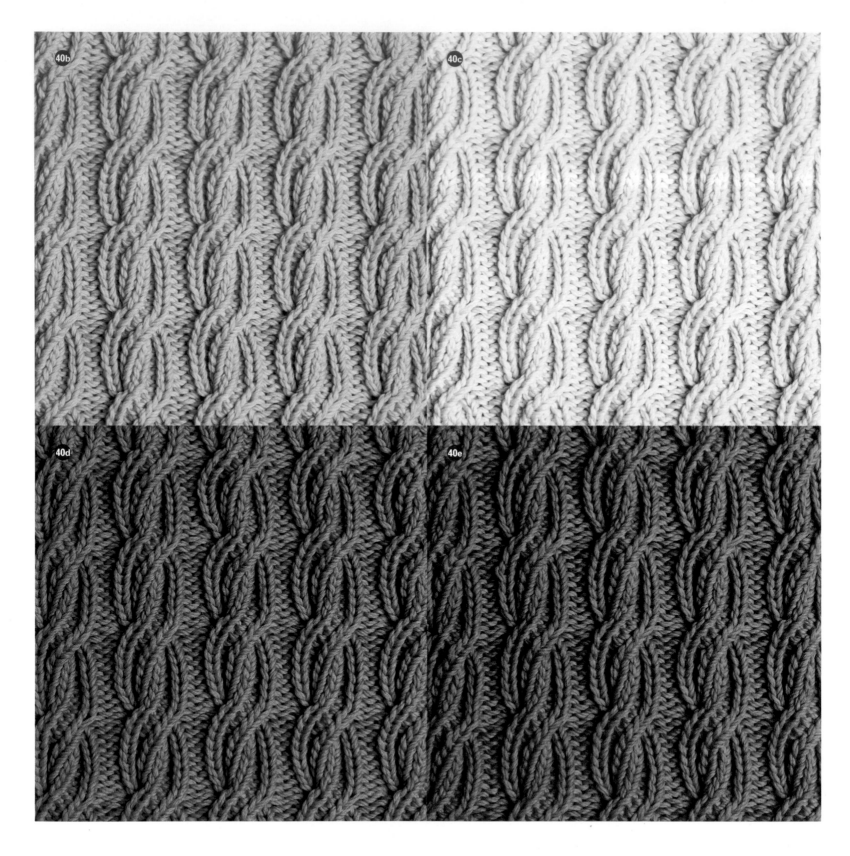

㊶ Apple

SIZE
8½oz in × 8½oz in(22cm × 22cm)

MATERIALS
1 pair US 9 (5.5mm/No. 5) needles

Single colorway (× 5⊞ ▣)
Rowan Cotton Rope
1¾oz (50g) balls

■ pink (A)		³⁄₅
▨ green (B)		¹⁄₁₀
□ white (C)		²⁄₅

³⁄₁₆in (5mm) beads
● black   6

□ K on RS, P on WS

KNIT
Thread 6 black beads onto B.
Cast on 37 sts and work until
chart row 50 completed.
Bind (cast) off sts.

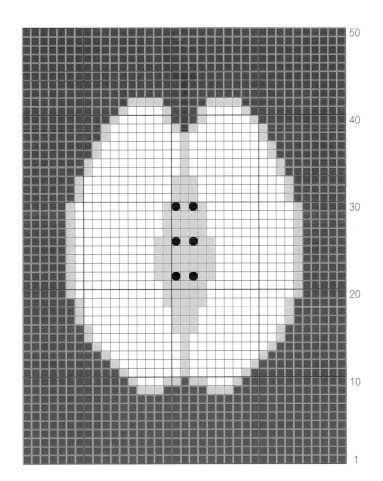

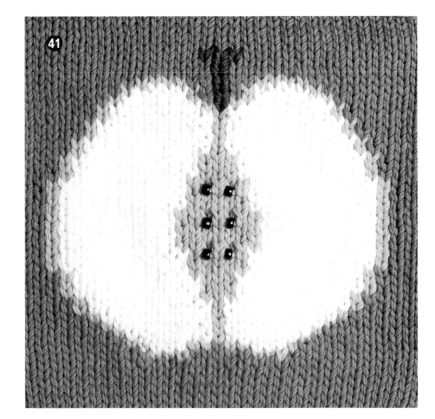

㊷ Orange

SIZE
8½in × 8½in (22cm × 22cm)

MATERIALS
1 pair US 9 (5.5mm/No. 5) needles

Single colorway (× 5⊞ ▣)
Rowan Cotton Rope
1¾oz (50g) balls

▨	blue (A)	³/₅
■	orange (B)	¹/₃
□	white (C)	¹/₅

³/₁₆in (5mm) beads
◌ white   6

□ K on RS, P on WS
⊟ P on RS, K on WS

KNIT
Thread 6 white beads onto B. Cast on 38 sts and work until chart row 49 completed. Bind (cast) off sts.

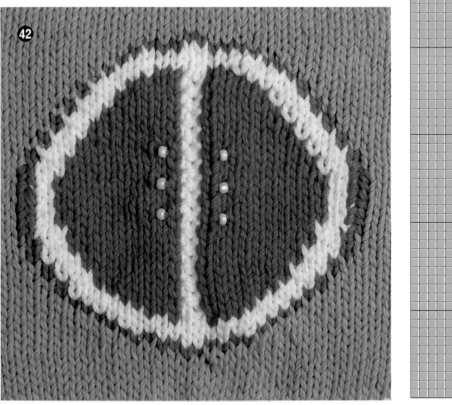

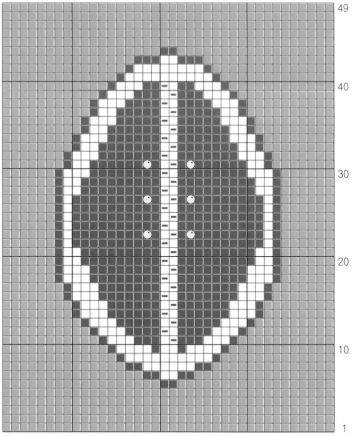

❹❸ Melon

SIZE
8½in × 8½in (22cm × 22cm)

MATERIALS
1 pair US 9 (5.5mm/No. 5) needles

Single colorway (× 5⊞ ▣)
Rowan Cotton Rope
1¾oz (50g) balls
☐ yellow (A)   ⁵/₇
▨ green (B)   ¹/₅
■ pink (C)   ¹/₇

Rowan Cotton Glace
1¾oz (50g) balls
■ dark green (D)   ¹/₂₅
(used double throughout)

³/₁₆in (5mm) beads
● black   16

☐ K on RS, P on WS

KNIT
Thread 16 black beads onto C.
Cast on 37 sts and work until
chart row 49 completed.
Bind (cast) off sts.

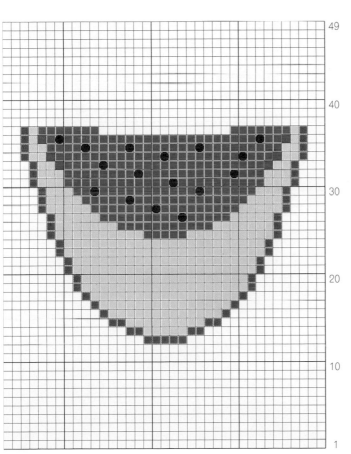

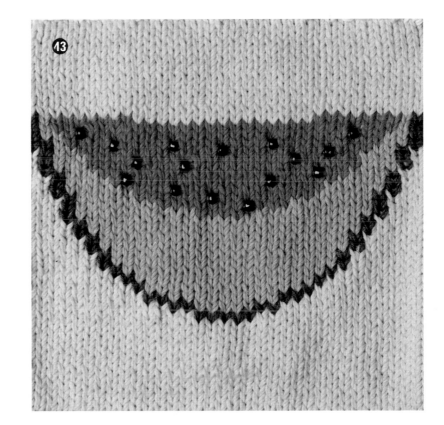

㊹ Kiwi

SIZE
8½in × 8½in (22cm × 22cm)

MATERIALS
1 pair US 9 (5.5mm/No. 5) needles

Single colorway (× 5⊞ ▣)
Rowan Cotton Rope
1¾oz (50g) balls
- ■ orange (A)   ⁵/₇
- ▨ green (B)   ⅓
- □ white (C)   ⅛

Rowan Cotton Glace
1¾oz (50g) balls
- ■ dark green (D)   ¹/₁₀
(used double throughout)

³/₁₆in (5mm) beads
- ● black   24

□ K on RS, P on WS

KNIT
Thread 24 black beads onto B.
Cast on 37 sts and work until
chart row 50 completed.
Bind (cast) off sts.

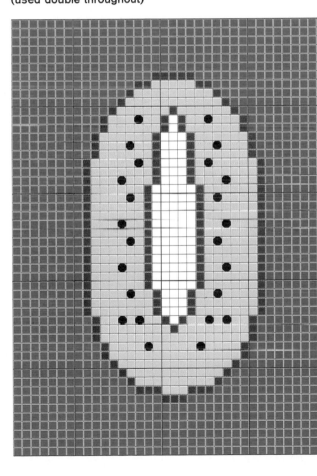

㊺ Peel

SIZE
8½in × 8½in (22cm × 22cm)

MATERIALS
1 pair US 9 (5.5mm/No. 5) needles

Single colorway (× 20▣)
Rowan Cotton Rope
1¾oz (50g) balls
- green   1

KNIT
Cast on 37 sts.
ROW 1 (RS): Knit.
ROW 2 (WS): P2, (K1, P3) 8 times,
K1, P2.
ROW 3 (RS): Knit.
ROW 4 (WS): Purl.
ROW 5 (RS): P1, (K3, P1) 8 times,
K3, P1.
ROW 6 (WS): Purl.
ROW 7 (RS): Knit.
Rep rows 2–7, 7 times more.
Rep row 2 once more.
(50 rows)
Bind (cast) off sts.

46 Fruity stripe

SIZE

8½in × 8½in (22cm × 22cm)

MATERIALS

1 pair US 9 (5.5mm/No. 5) needles

46a First colorway (× 4■)

Rowan Cotton Rope
1¾oz (50g) balls

yellow (A)	½
purple (B)	½

46b Second colorway (× 4■)

Rowan Cotton Rope
1¾oz (50g) balls

orange (A)	½
blue (B)	½

46c Third colorway (× 4■)

Rowan Cotton Rope
1¾oz (50g) balls

pink (A)	½
yellow (B)	½

46d Fourth colorway (× 4■)

Rowan Cotton Rope
1¾oz (50g) balls

purple (A)	½
blue (B)	½

KNIT

Cast on 37 sts.
Note: Do not cut off yarns. Carry them up the side of the work.
ROW 1 (RS): A, knit.
ROW 2 (WS): A, purl.
ROW 3 (RS): A, knit.
ROW 4 (WS): B, purl.
ROW 5 (RS): B, knit.
ROW 6 (WS): K1B, (P1B, K1B) 18 times.
ROW 7 (RS): B, knit.
ROW 8 (WS): A, purl.
ROW 9 (RS): A, knit.
ROW 10 (WS): A, purl.
Transfer sts back onto LH needle so the WS of the work is facing you again.
ROW 11 (WS): B, purl.
ROW 12 (RS): B, knit.
ROW 13 (WS): K1B, (P1B, K1B) 18 times.
ROW 14 (RS): B, knit.
Transfer sts back onto LH needle so the RS of the work is facing you again.
Rep rows 1–14 twice more, including the transferring of sts.
Rep rows 1–10 once more.
(52 rows)
Bind (cast) off sts.

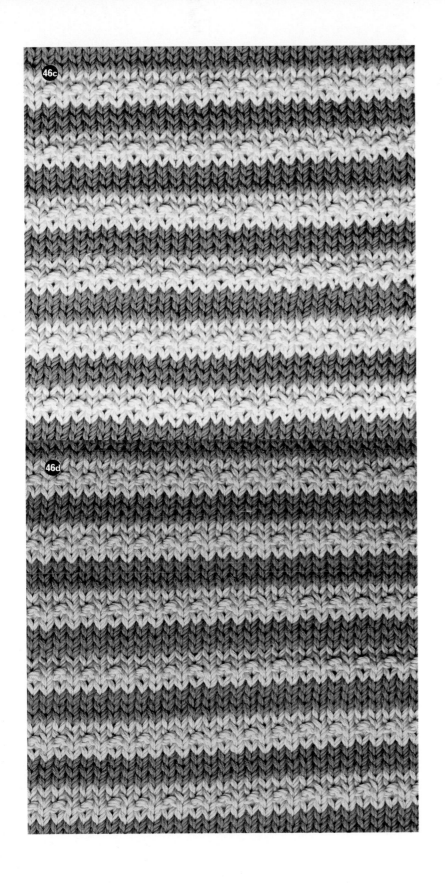

modern mineral

Nature provides us with a vast range of design possibilities and for this particular design I focussed on geology and natural materials. Ideas were sourced from fossils, geological specimens, and minerals. The colors are sympathetic to the theme and the muted range of chocolate, stone, and silver-gray echo the earth's colors. The addition of lurex threads and sparkling beads are included to suggest mica as found naturally in rocks and pebbles. The whole color scheme has been carefully selected for its ambience and serenity.

SIZE

78in × 54in (195cm × 135cm)

MATERIALS

1 pair US 5 (3.75mm/No. 9) needles
2 circular US 2–3 (3.00mm/No. 11) needles 32in (80cm) length
2 circular US 5 (3.75mm/No. 9) needles 39in (100cm) length
Cable needle

Yarn

Rowan Wool Cotton DK
1³⁄₄oz (50g) balls

stone	12
chocolate	7
black	6
gray	7

Rowan Yorkshire Tweed DK
1³⁄₄oz (50g) balls

brown tweed	3
cream tweed	2

Rowan Lurex Shimmer
1oz (25g) balls

silver	2

(used double throughout)

bronze	2

(used double throughout)
Quantities given for individual squares are approximate fractions of a ball.

Beads

¹⁄₈in (3mm) beads

silver	72
white	72

GAUGE (TENSION)

24sts and 32 rows to 4in (10cm) measured over stockinette (stocking) stitch using US 5 (3.75mm/No. 9) needles.

ABBREVIATIONS

See page 127.

FINISHING

The sizes given for the finished afghan and individual squares are approximate. The number of stitches in a row, and the number of rows in a square differ in some instances. Therefore, when sewing pieces together, ease the extra stitches or rows into the adjoining square.

Press the individual squares using a damp cloth and a warm iron. Sew the squares together, joining bound (cast) off edge of one square to the cast-on edge of the next square, easing in stitches, if necessary, to form vertical strips. Sew the vertical strips together, easing in rows, if necessary, to create one block.

Edging

MATERIALS

2 circular US 2–3 (3.00mm/No. 11) needles 32in (80cm) length
2 circular US 5 (3.75mm/No. 9) needles 39in (100cm) length

Yarn

Rowan Wool Cotton
1³⁄₄oz (50g) balls

black (A)	2¹⁄₂

Rowan Yorkshire Tweed DK
1³⁄₄oz (50g) balls

brown tweed (B)	³⁄₅

KNIT

With RS facing and using a US 2–3 (3.00mm/No. 11) circular needle and A, pick up and knit 471 sts along the RH edge of the afghan.
Beg with a WS row, cont to work in garter stitch (knit every row) for 5 rows, inc 1 st at each end of all WS rows (477 sts).
Change to US 5 (3.75mm/No. 9) circular needle.
ROW 6 (RS): A, knit.
Push sts to other end of circular needle so that the RS is facing again.
ROW 7 (RS): Using B, inc once into first st, (K1, P1) to last 2 sts, inc once into next st, K1 (479 sts).
ROW 8 (WS): B, purl.
Change to US 2–3 (3.00mm/No. 11) circular needle.
ROW 9 (RS): Using A, inc once into first st, (K1, P1) to last 2 sts, inc once into next st, K1 (481 sts).
ROW 10 (WS): A, purl.
Using A, bind (cast) off sts purlwise.
Rep for LH edge of the afghan.
With RS facing and A, pick up and knit 327 sts along bottom edge of the afghan.
Rep edging as for RH and LH edges.
Rep for top edge of afghan.
Neatly sew border edges together.

Order of squares

47	53	56	50b	47	50b	57	53	47
48	54	52a	54	55	54	52a	54	48
49	52b	47	53	51	53	47	52b	51
52a	54	55	54	48	54	55	54	52a
47	53	56	50b	47	50b	57	53	47
48	54	50a	54	55	54	50a	54	48
51	55	47	53	49	53	47	55	49
48	54	52a	54	55	54	52a	54	48
47	53	56	52b	47	52b	57	53	47
50a	54	55	54	48	54	55	54	50a
49	50b	47	53	51	53	47	50b	51
48	54	50a	54	55	54	50a	54	48
47	53	56	52b	47	52b	57	53	47

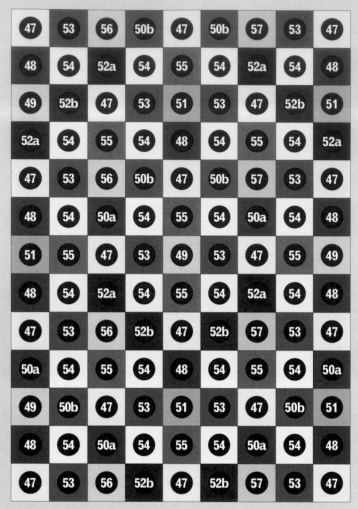

QUANTITY OF SQUARES

㊼ Fossil	18
㊽ Bronze stripe	10
㊾ Flint 1	4
㊿ Mineral stripe 1	
(50a) First colorway	6
(50b) Second colorway	6
(51) Flint 2	5
(52) Mineral stripe 2	
(52a) First colorway	6
(52b) Second colorway	6
(53) Slate	14
(54) Barnacles	24
(55) Strata	10
(56) Stone 1	4
(57) Stone 2	4

㊼ Fossil

SIZE

6in × 6in (15cm × 15cm)

MATERIALS

1 pair US 5 (3.75mm/No. 9) needles
Cable needle

Single colorway (× 18■)
Rowan Wool Cotton DK
$1\frac{3}{4}$oz (50g) balls
stone (A) $\frac{2}{5}$

Rowan Yorkshire Tweed DK
$1\frac{3}{4}$oz (50g) balls
brown tweed (B) $\frac{1}{25}$

KNIT

Cast on 38 sts.
ROW 1 (RS) (INC): P2A, (using A, inc once into each of next 4 sts, P1A, K1A, P2A, K1A, P1A) 3 times, using A, inc once into each of next 4 sts, P2A (54 sts).
ROW 2 (WS): K2A, (P8A, K1A, P1A, K2A, P1A, K1A) 3 times, P8A, K2A.
ROW 3 (RS): P2A, (K8A, P1A, yb, sl1p, yf, P2A, yb, sl1p, yf, P1A) 3 times, K8A, P2A.
ROW 4 (WS): As row 2.
ROWS 5–6: Rep rows 3–4.
ROW 7 (RS): P2B, (c8bB, P1B, yb, sl1p, yf, P2B, yb, sl1p, yf, P1B) 3 times, c8bB, P2B.
ROW 8 (WS): As row 2.
ROWS 9–14: Rep rows 3–4, 3 times.
ROW 15 (RS): P2B, (c8fB, P1B, yb, sl1p, yf, P2B, yb, sl1p, yf, P1B) 3 times, c8fB, P2B.
ROWS 16–22: Rep rows 8–14.
ROWS 23–38: Rep rows 7–22.
ROWS 39–51: Rep rows 7–19.
ROW 52 (WS) (DEC): K2A, (P2togA 4 times, K1A, P1A, K2A, P1A, K1A) 3 times, P2togA 4 times, K2A (38 sts).
Bind (cast) off sts.

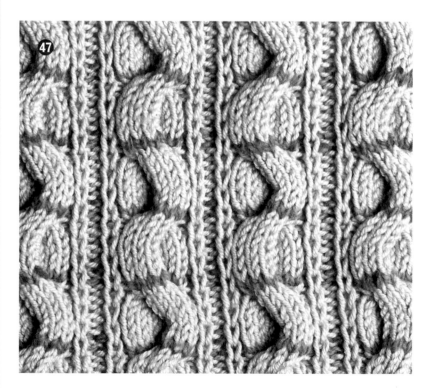

❽ Bronze stripe

SIZE
6in × 6in (15cm × 15cm)

MATERIALS
1 pair US 5 (3.75mm/No. 9)
  needles

Single colorway (× 10◼)
Rowan Wool Cotton DK
1¾oz (50g) balls
  chocolate (A)   ⅓

Rowan Lurex Shimmer
1oz (25g) balls
  bronze (B)   ³⁄₂₅
(used double throughout)

KNIT
Cast on 38 sts using A.
Working in plain stockinette
(stocking) stitch (knit on RS rows
and purl on WS rows), and beg
with a RS row, cont in stripe patt
as folls:
ROWS 1–3: **A.**
ROWS 4–7: **B.**
ROWS 8–11: **A.**
Rep rows 4–11, 4 times more.
Rep rows 4–10 once more.
(50 rows).
Bind (cast) off sts.

❾ Flint 1

SIZE
6in × 6in (15cm × 15cm)

MATERIALS
1 pair US 5 (3.75mm/No. 9)
  needles

Single colorway (× 4⊞ ◼)
Rowan Wool Cotton DK
1¾oz (50g) balls
☐ stone (A)   ⅙
◼ gray (B)   ⅐
◼ black (C)   ¹⁄₂₅

⅛in (3mm) beads
◉ silver   8

☐ K on RS, P on WS

KNIT
Thread 8 silver beads onto C.
Cast on 38 sts and work until
chart row 50 completed.
Bind (cast) off sts.

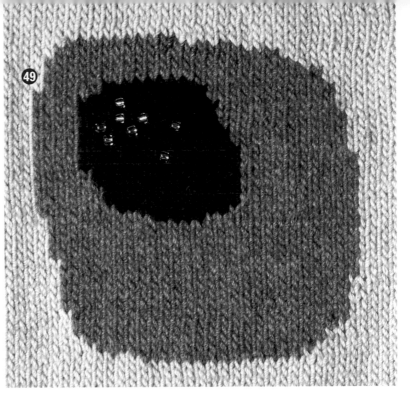

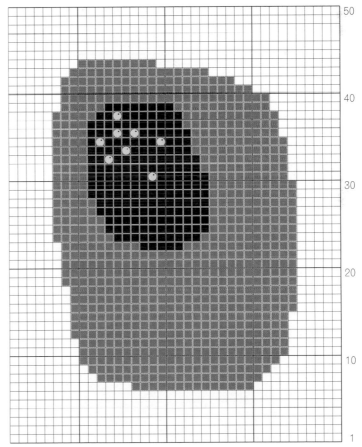

㊿ Mineral stripe 1

SIZE
6in × 6in (15cm × 15cm)

MATERIALS
1 pair US 5 (3.75mm/No. 9)
  needles

⁵⁰ᵃ First colorway (× 6■)
Rowan Wool Cotton DK
1³⁄₄oz (50g) balls
  chocolate (A)   ¹⁄₄
  stone (D)   ¹⁄₂₅

Rowan Yorkshire Tweed DK
1³⁄₄oz (50g) balls
  brown tweed (B)   ¹⁄₂₅
  cream tweed (E)   ¹⁄₁₆

Rowan Lurex Shimmer
1oz (25g) balls
  bronze (C)   ¹⁄₂₅
(used double throughout)

⁵⁰ᵇ Second colorway (× 6■)
Rowan Wool Cotton DK
1³⁄₄oz (50g) balls
  black (A)   ¹⁄₄
  gray (B)   ¹⁄₂₅
  stone (D)   ¹⁄₂₅

Rowan Yorkshire Tweed
1³⁄₄oz (50g) balls
  cream tweed (E)   ¹⁄₁₆

Rowan Lurex Shimmer
  silver (C)   ¹⁄₂₅
(used double throughout)

KNIT
Cast on 38 sts using A.
Working in plain stockinette
(stocking) stitch (knit on RS rows
and purl on WS rows), and beg
with a RS row, cont in stripe patt
as folls:
ROWS 1–24: **A.**
ROW 25–28: **B.**
ROWS 29–30: **A.**
ROW 31: **B.**
ROW 32: **C.**
ROWS 33–34: **D.**
ROWS 35–40: **E.**
ROWS 41–43: **A.**
ROWS 44–45: **D.**
ROW 46: **A.**
ROWS 47–49: **B.**
(49 rows)
Bind (cast) off sts.

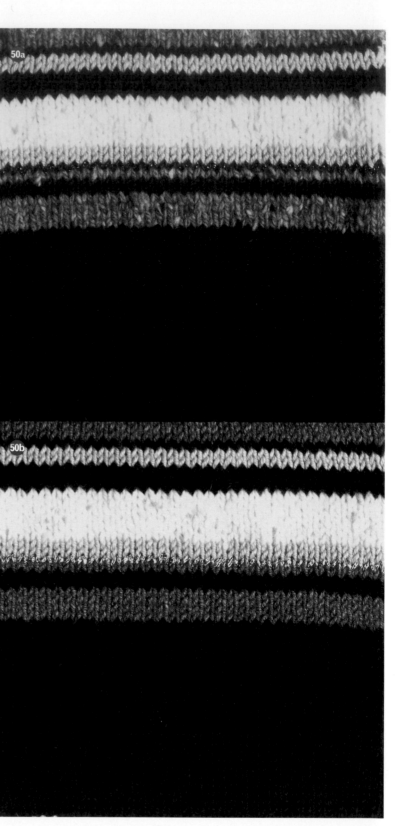

50a

50b

(51) Flint 2

SIZE

6in × 6in (15cm × 15cm)

MATERIALS

1 pair US 5 (3.75mm/No. 9) needles

Single colorway (× 5 ▦ ▣)

Rowan Wool Cotton DK

1¾oz (50g) balls

□ stone (A)	1/6
■ gray (B)	1/7
■ black (C)	1/25

⅛in (3mm) beads

◌ silver	8

□ K on RS, P on WS

KNIT

Thread 8 silver beads onto C. Cast on 38 sts and work until chart row 50 completed. Bind (cast) off sts.

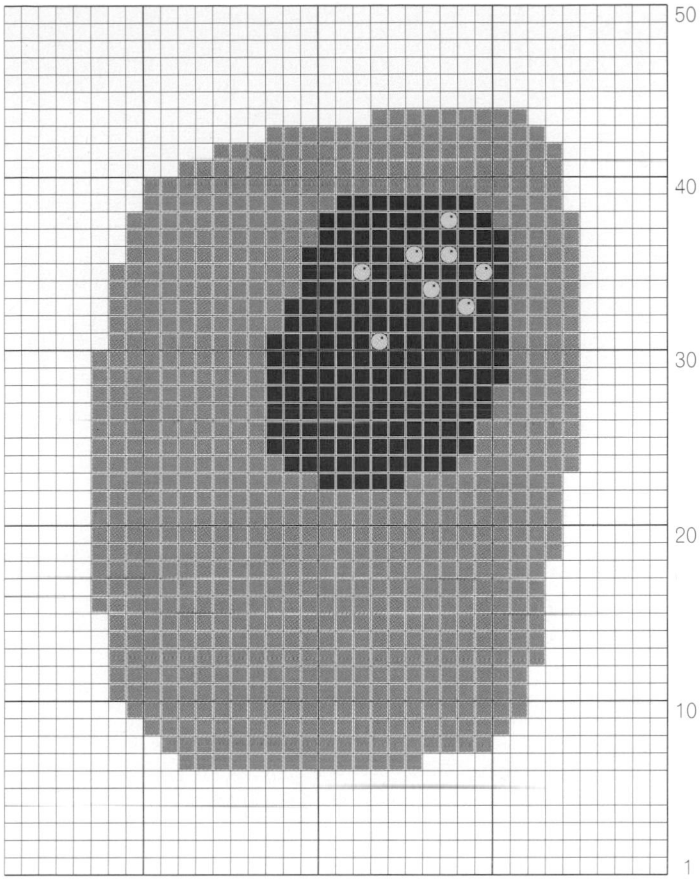

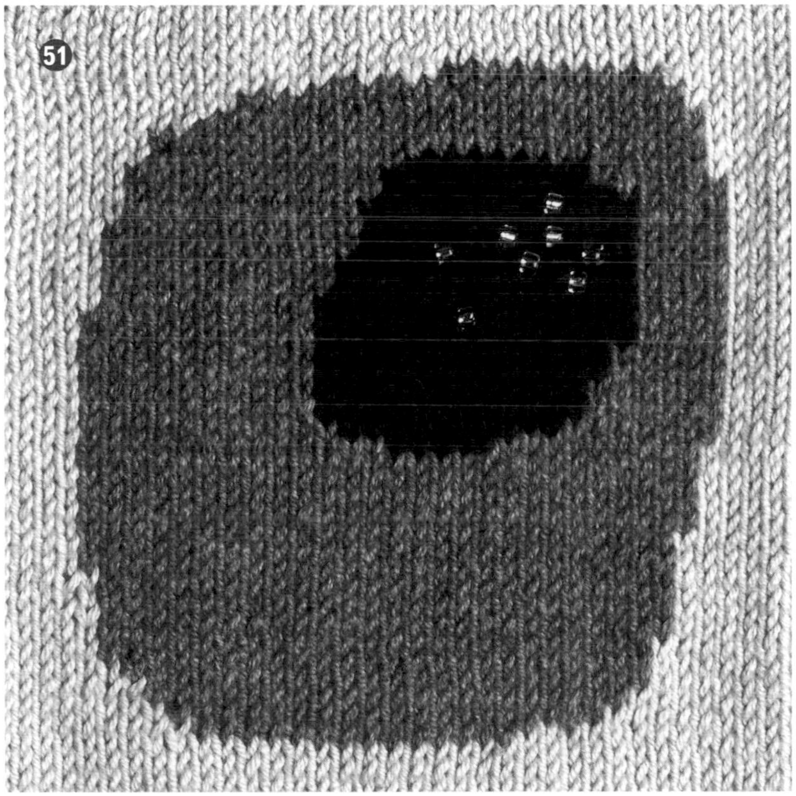

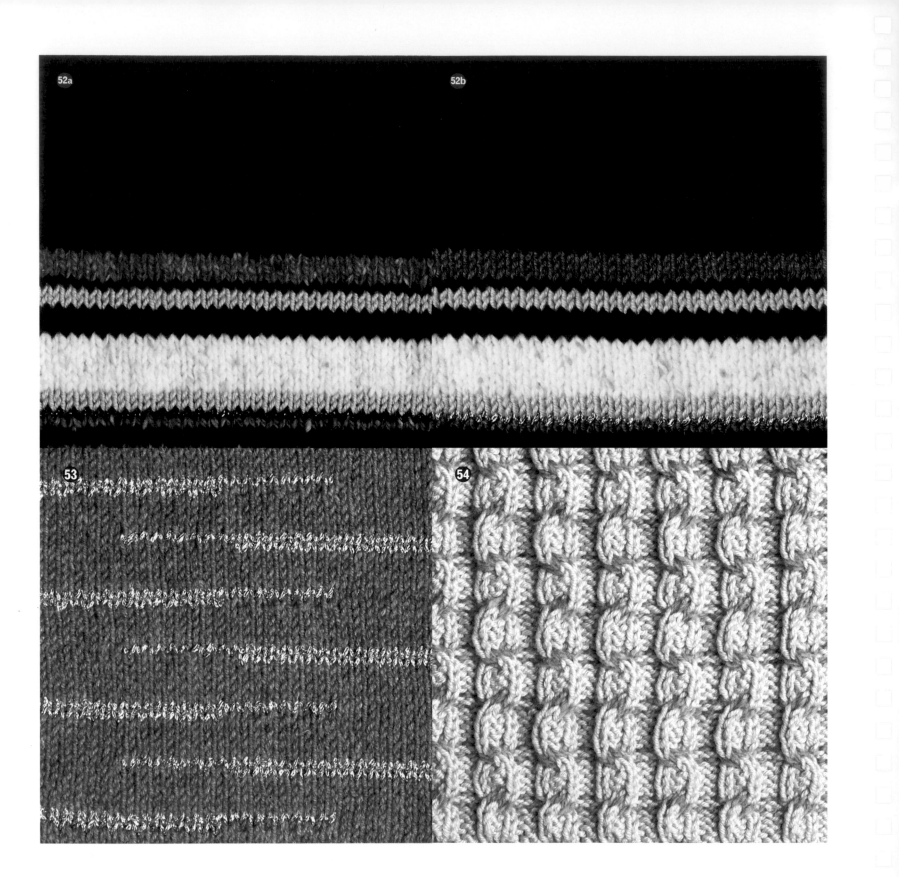

52 Mineral stripe 2

SIZE

6in × 6in (15cm × 15cm)

MATERIALS

1 pair US 5 (3.75mm/No. 9)
  needles

52a First colorway (× 6■)

Rowan Yorkshire Tweed DK
1¾oz (50g) balls
  brown tweed (A)   ¹⁄₂₅
  cream tweed (E)   ¹⁄₁₆

Rowan Wool Cotton DK
1¾oz (50g) balls
  chocolate (B)   ¼
  stone (D)   ¹⁄₂₅

Rowan Lurex Shimmer
1oz (25g) balls
  bronze (C)   ¹⁄₂₅
(used double throughout)

52b Second colorway (× 6■)

Rowan Yorkshire Tweed DK
1¾oz (50g) balls
  cream tweed (E)   ¹⁄₁₆

Rowan Wool Cotton DK
1¾oz (50g) balls
  gray (A)   ¹⁄₂₅
  black (B)   ¼
  stone (D)   ¹⁄₂₅

Rowan Lurex Shimmer
1oz (25g) balls
  silver (C)   ¹⁄₂₅
(used double throughout)

KNIT

Cast on 38 sts using A.
Working in plain stockinette
(stocking) stitch (knit on RS rows
and purl on WS rows), and beg
with a RS row, cont in stripe patt
as folls:
ROWS 1–4: **A.**
ROWS 5–6: **B.**
ROW 7: **A.**
ROW 8: **C.**
ROWS 9–10: **D.**
ROWS 11–16: **E.**
ROWS 17–19: **B.**
ROWS 20–21: **D.**
ROW 22: **B.**
ROWS 23–25: **A.**
ROWS 26–49: **B.**
(49 rows)
Bind (cast) off sts.

53 Slate

SIZE

6in × 6in (15cm × 15cm)

MATERIALS

1 pair US 5 (3.75mm/No. 9)
  needles

Single colorway (× 14■)

Rowan Wool Cotton DK
1¾oz (50g) balls
  gray (A)   ⅓

Rowan Lurex Shimmer
1oz (25g) balls
  silver (B)   ³⁄₂₅
(used double throughout)

KNIT

Cast on 37 sts using A.
ROW 1 (RS): **A, knit.**
ROW 2 (WS): **A, purl.**
ROWS 3–4: **Rep rows 1–2.**
ROW 5: **A, knit.**
ROW 6 (WS): **P18B, P19A.**
ROW 7 (RS): **K10A, K27B.**
ROW 8 (WS): **A, purl.**
ROWS 9–10: **Rep rows 1–2.**
ROW 11 (RS): **A, knit.**
ROW 12 (WS): **P19A, P18B.**
ROW 13 (RS): **K27B, K10A.**
ROW 14 (WS): **A, purl.**
ROWS 15–16: **Rep rows 1–2.**
ROWS 17–40: **Rep rows 5–16 twice.**
ROWS 41–47: **Rep rows 5–11.**
ROW 48 (WS): **A, purl.**
ROWS 49–50: **Rep rows 1–2 once more.**
(50 rows)
Bind (cast) off sts.

54 Barnacles

SIZE

6in × 6in (15cm × 15cm)

MATERIALS

1 pair US 5 (3.75mm/No. 9)
  needles
Cable needle

Single colorway (× 24■)

Rowan Wool Cotton DK
1¾oz (50g) balls
  stone (A)   ⅓

Rowan Yorkshire Tweed DK
1¾oz (50g) balls
  brown tweed (B)   ¹⁄₂₅

KNIT

Cast on 38 sts using A.
ROW 1 (RS) (INC): **P3A, (using A, inc once into each of next 2 sts, P3A) 7 times (52 sts).**
ROW 2 (WS): **K3A, (P4A, K3A) 7 times.**
ROW 3 (RS): **P3A, (K1A, P2A, K1A, P3A) 7 times.**
ROW 4 (WS): **K3A, (P1A, K2A, P1A, K3A) 7 times.**
ROW 5 (RS): **P3A, (K4A, P3A) 7 times.**
ROW 6 (WS): **K3B, (P4B, K3B) 7 times.**
ROW 7 (RS): **P3A, (c4bA, P3A) 7 times.**
ROW 8 (WS): **As row 2.**
ROWS 9–10: **Rep rows 3–4.**
ROW 11 (RS): **As row 5.**
ROW 12 (WS): **As row 6.**
ROW 13 (RS): **P3A, (c4fA, P3A) 7 times.**
ROW 14 (WS): **As row 2.**
Rep rows 3–14, 3 times more.
Rep row 3 once more.
NEXT ROW (WS) (DEC): **P3A, (using A, P2tog twice, P3A) 7 times (38 sts).**
(52 rows).
Bind (cast) off sts.

55 Strata

SIZE
6in × 6in (15cm × 15cm)

MATERIALS
1 pair US 5 (3.75mm/No. 9)
    needles

Single colorway (× 10 ■)
Rowan Wool Cotton DK
1¾oz (50g) balls
    black (A)   ¼

Rowan Yorkshire Tweed DK
1¾oz (50g) balls
    brown tweed (B)   ¹⁄₁₆

KNIT
Cast on 37 sts using A.
ROW 1 (RS): A, knit.
ROW 2 (WS): A, purl.
ROWS 3–4: Rep rows 1–2.
ROW 5 (RS): K1B, (P1B, K1B) 18
times.
ROW 6 (WS): B, purl.
ROW 7 (RS): K1A, (P1A, K1A) 18
times.
ROW 8 (WS): A, purl.
Rep rows 1–8, 5 times more.
Rep rows 1–2 once more.
(50 rows)
Bind (cast) off sts.

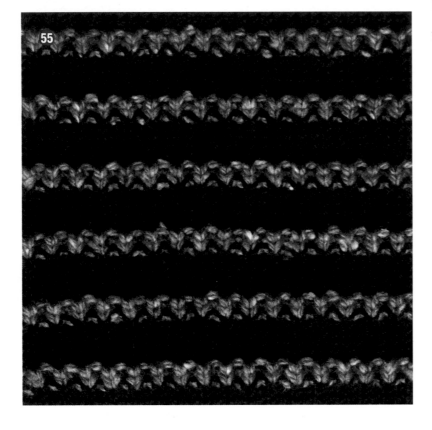

55

56 Stone 1

SIZE
6in × 6in (15cm × 15cm)

MATERIALS
1 pair US 5 (3.75mm/No. 9)
    needles

Single colorway (× 4 ⊞ ■)
Rowan Wool Cotton DK
1¾oz (50g) balls
    ☐ stone (A)   ⅕
    ■ chocolate (C)   ¹⁄₂₅

Rowan Yorkshire Tweed DK
1¾oz (50g) balls
    ▨ brown tweed (B)   ¹⁄₁₂

⅛in (3mm) beads
    ⊙ white   9

☐ K on RS, P on WS

KNIT
Thread 9 white beads onto C.
Cast on 38 sts and work until
chart row 49 completed.
Bind (cast) off sts.

57 Stone 2

SIZE
6in × 6in (15cm × 15cm)

MATERIALS
1 pair US 5 (3.75mm/No. 9)
   needles

Single colorway (× 4⊞ ▣)
Rowan Wool Cotton DK
1¾oz (50g) balls
☐ stone (A)   ⅕
■ chocolate (C)   ¹⁄₂₅

Rowan Yorkshire Tweed DK
1¾oz (50g) balls
▨ brown tweed (B)   ¹⁄₁₂

⅛in (3mm) beads
⊙ white   9

☐ K on RS, P on WS

KNIT
Thread 9 white beads onto C.
Cast on 38 sts and work until
chart row 49 completed.
Bind (cast) off sts.

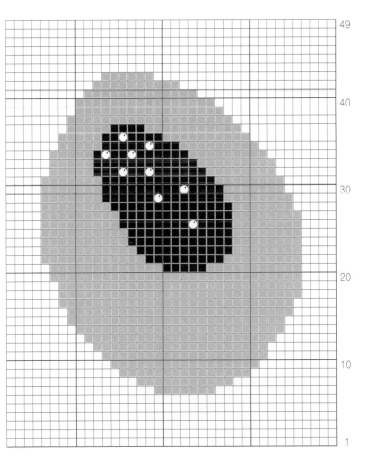

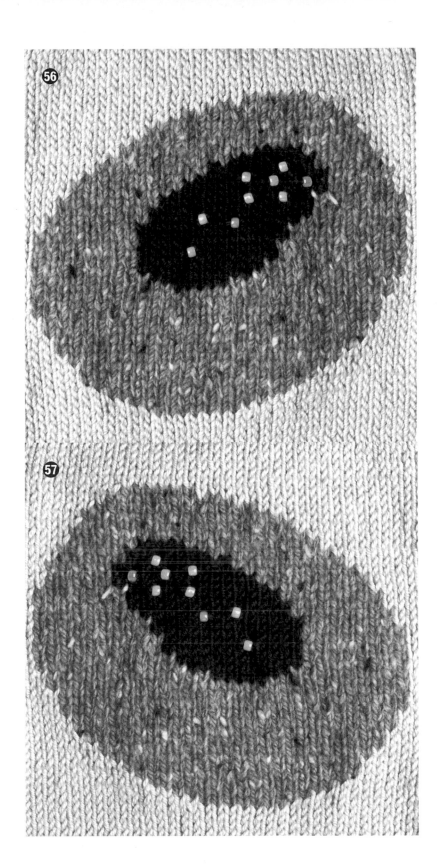

playmat

Playmat combines a learning tool with a soft furnishing. The numbers, letters, and geometric shapes are included as an aid to a child's learning skills, and the afghan itself provides warmth and comfort for the infant. This unisex design uses soft, sugary colors to create a welcoming environment for both mother and baby.

SIZE
49in × 49in (123cm × 123cm)

MATERIALS
1 pair US 6 (4.00mm/No. 8)
needles
2 circular US 3 (3.25mm/No. 10)
needles 39in (100cm) length
cable needle

Yarn
Rowan All Seasons Cotton
1³⁄₄oz (50g) balls

blue	7
dark pink	1
green	6
cream	2
pale pink	6
yellow	6

Quantities given for individual
squares are approximate fractions
of a ball

GAUGE (TENSION)
19 sts and 27 rows to 4in (10cm)
measured over stockinette
(stocking) stitch using US 6
(4.00mm/No. 8) needles.

NOTE
Single stitch outlines on squares
59, 61, 62, 63, 67a, 67a, 68, 69a,
69b, 70a, 70b and 71 can be
Swiss–darned after knitting (see
page 122).

ABBREVIATIONS
See page 127.

FINISHING
The sizes given for the finished
afghan and individual squares are
approximate. The number of
stitches in a row, and the number
of rows in a square differ in some
instances. Therefore, when sewing
pieces together, ease the extra
stitches or rows into the adjoining
square.

Press the individual squares
using a damp cloth and a warm
iron. Sew the squares together,
joining bound- (cast-) off edge of
one square to the cast-on edge of
the next square, easing in stitches,
if necessary, to form vertical
strips. Sew the vertical strips
together, easing in rows, if
necessary, to create one block.

Edging

MATERIALS
2 circular US 3 (3.25mm/No. 10)
needles 39in (100cm) length

Yarn
Rowan All Seasons Cotton
1³⁄₄oz (50g) balls

blue (A)	³⁄₅
pale pink (B)	³⁄₅

KNIT
With RS facing and A, pick up and
knit 254 sts along the RH edge of
the afghan.
Beg with a WS row, work as folls:
ROW 1 (WS): A, inc once into first
st, K to last 2 sts, inc once into
next st, K1 (256 sts).
ROW 2 (RS): A, purl.
ROWS 3–4. Rep rows 1–2 (258 sts).
Using B, bind (cast) off sts
knitwise.
Rep for LH edge of the afghan.
With RS facing and B, pick up and
knit 249 sts along bottom edge of
the afghan.
Beg with a WS row, work as folls:
ROW 1 (WS): B, inc once into first
st, K to last 2 sts, inc once into
next st, K1 (251 sts).
ROW 2 (RS): B, purl.
ROWS 3–4: Rep rows 1–2 (253 sts).
Using A, bind (cast) off sts,
knitwise.
Rep for top edge of the afghan.
Neatly sew border edges together.

Order of squares

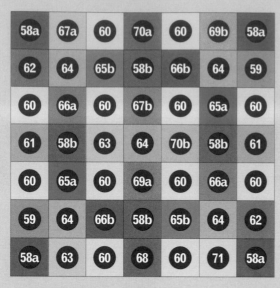

58a	67a	60	70a	60	69b	58a
62	64	65b	58b	66b	64	59
60	66a	60	67b	60	65a	60
61	58b	63	64	70b	58b	61
60	65a	60	69a	60	66a	60
59	64	66b	58b	65b	64	62
58a	63	60	68	60	71	58a

QUANTITY OF SQUARES

58 Bobble grid
  58a First colorway — 4
  58b Second colorway — 4
59 One
60 Baby doll stripe — 12
61 Two — 2
62 Three — 2
63 The letter d — 2
64 Dolly — 5
65 Triangle
  65a First colorway — 2
  65b Second colorway — 2
66 Circle
  66a First colorway — 2
  66b Second colorway — 2
67 The letter a
  67a First colorway — 1
  67b Second colorway — 1
68 The letter e — 1
69 The letter c
  69a First colorway — 1
  69b Second colorway — 1
70 The letter b
  70a First colorway — 1
  70b Second colorway — 1
71 The letter f — 1

58 Bobble grid

SIZE
7in × 7in (18cm × 18cm)

MATERIALS
1 pair US 6 (4.00mm/No. 8) needles

58a First colorway (× 4 ■)
Rowan All Seasons Cotton
1¾oz (50g) balls
  blue (A)   ½
  pale pink (B)   ¹⁄₂₅
  green (C)   ¹⁄₂₅

58b Second colorway (× 4 ■)
Rowan All Seasons Cotton
1¾oz (50g) balls
  blue (A)   ½
  dark pink (B)   ¹⁄₂₅
  green (C)   ¹⁄₂₅

KNIT
Cast on 37 sts.
ROW 1 (RS): A, purl.
ROW 2 (WS): K6A, (P1A, K5A) 5 times, K1A.

ROW 3 (RS): P6A, (yb, sl1p, yf, P5A) 5 times, P1A.
ROW 4 (WS): As row 2.
ROWS 5–6: Rep rows 3–4.
ROW 7 (RS): P3A, (mbA, P2A, yb, sl1p, yf, P2A) 5 times, mbA, P3A.
ROW 8 (WS): As row 2.
ROW 9 (RS): K6B, (keeping yarn at back of work, sl1p, K5B) 5 times, K1B.
ROW 10 (WS): K6B, (P1B, K5B) 5 times, K1B.
ROWS 11–14: Rep rows 3–4 twice.
ROWS 15–16: Rep rows 7–8.
ROW 17 (RS): K6C, (keeping yarn at back of work, sl1p, K5C) 5 times, K1C.
ROW 18 (WS): K6C, (P1C, K5C) 5 times, K1C.
Rep rows 11–16 once more.
Rep rows 9–18 once more.
Rep rows 3–16 once more.
Rep rows 3–4 once more.
(50 rows)
Bind (cast) off sts.

58a

❺❾ One

SIZE
7in × 7in (18cm × 18cm)

MATERIALS
1 pair US 6 (4.00mm/No. 8)
    needles

Single colorway (× 2⊞ ▣)
Rowan All Seasons Cotton
1³⁄₄oz (50g) balls

⬜	green (A)	¹⁄₂
🟪	dark pink (B)	¹⁄₂₅

⬜ K on RS, P on WS
⊟ P on WS, K on RS

KNIT
Cast on 37 sts and work until
chart row 49 completed.
Bind (cast) off sts.

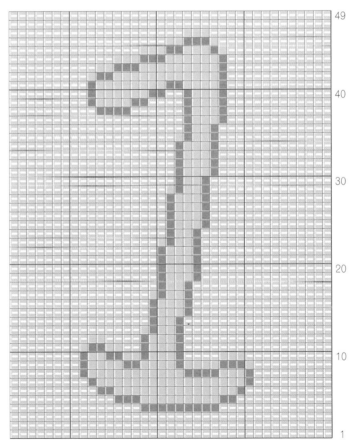

⓺⓪ Baby doll stripe

SIZE
7in × 7in (18cm × 18cm)

MATERIALS
1 pair US 6 (4.00mm/No. 8)
  needles

Single colorway (× 12■)
Rowan All Seasons Cotton
1¾oz (50g) balls

cream (A)	⅙
blue (B)	⅐
pale pink (C)	⅕

KNIT
Cast on 37 sts using A.
ROW 1 (RS): **A**, knit.
ROW 2 (WS): **A**, purl.
ROW 3 (RS): **B**, knit.
ROW 4 (WS): **B**, purl.
ROW 5 (RS): **K1B**, (P1B, K1B) 18 times.
ROW 6 (WS): **K1B**, (P1B, K1B) 18 times.
ROWS 7–8: Rep rows 1–2.
ROW 9 (RS): **C**, knit.
ROW 10 (WS): **C**, purl.
ROW 11 (RS): **K1C**, (P1C, K1C) 18 times.
ROW 12 (WS): **K1C**, (P1C, K1C) 18 times.
Rep rows 1–12, 3 times more.
Rep rows 1–2 once more.
(50 rows)
Bind (cast) off sts.

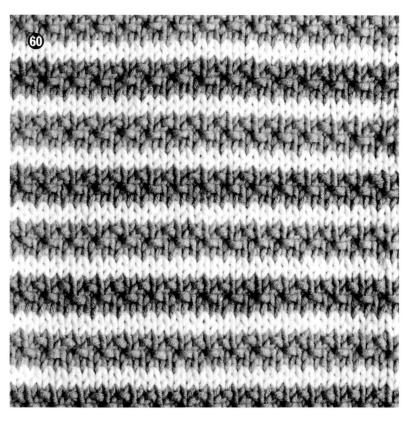

⓺① Two

SIZE
7in × 7in (18cm × 18cm)

MATERIALS
1 pair US 6 (4.00mm/No. 8)
  needles

Single colorway (× 2⊞ ■)
Rowan All Seasons Cotton
1¾oz (50g) balls

☐ yellow (A)	½
▦ blue (B)	½₅

☐ K on RS, P on WS
⊟ P on RS, K on WS

KNIT
Cast on 37 sts and work until chart row 50 completed.
Bind (cast) off sts.

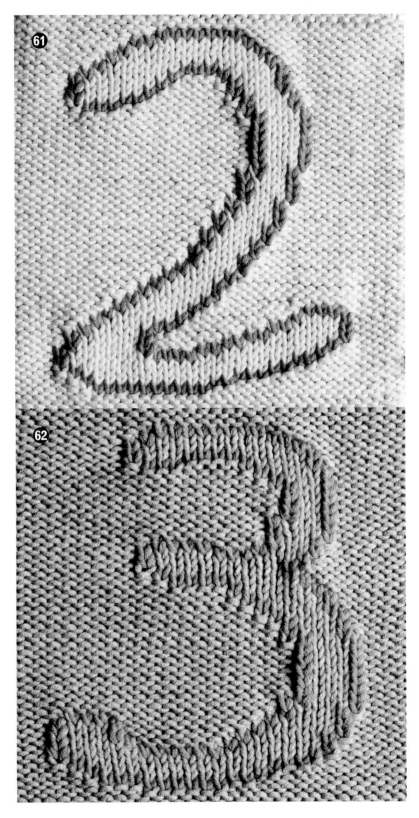

⓺ Three

SIZE
7in × 7in (18cm × 18cm)

MATERIALS
1 pair US 6 (4.00mm/No. 8)
  needles

Single colorway (× 2⊞ ▣)
Rowan All Seasons Cotton
1¾oz (50g) balls

☐ green (A)	½
■ dark pink (B)	½₂₅

☐ K on RS, P on WS
⊟ P on RS, K on WS

KNIT
Cast on 37 sts and work until
chart row 49 completed.
Bind (cast) off sts.

⑥③ The letter d

SIZE
7in × 7in (18cm × 18cm)

MATERIALS
1 pair US 6 (4.00mm/No. 8)
 needles

Single colorway (× 2⊞ ▣)
Rowan All Seasons Cotton
1¾oz (50g) balls
☐ yellow (A)   ½
▣ blue (B)   ¹⁄₂₅

☐ K on RS, P on WS
⊟ P on RS, K on WS

KNIT
Cast on 37 sts and work until
chart row 49 completed.
Bind (cast) off sts.

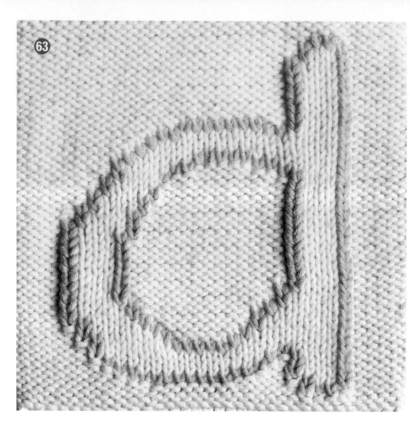

⑥④ Dolly

SIZE
7in × 7in (18cm × 18cm)

MATERIALS
1 pair US 6 (4.00mm/No. 8)
 needles
Cable needle

Single colorway (× 5▣)
Rowan All Seasons Cotton
1¾oz (50g) balls
 pale pink   ³⁄₅

KNIT
Cast on 37 sts.
ROW 1 (RS) (INC): (K1, P1) twice, [K1,
inc once into each of the next 3
sts, (K1, P1) twice] 4 times,
K1 (49 sts).
ROW 2 (WS): K1, P1, K1, (P10, K1)
4 times, P1, K1.
ROW 3 (RS): (K1, P1) twice, (K8, P1,
K1, P1) 4 times, K1.
ROW 4 (WS): As row 2.
ROWS 5–8: Rep rows 3–4
twice.
ROW 9 (RS): (K1, P1) twice, (c8b, P1,
K1, P1) 4 times, K1.
ROW 10 (WS): As row 2.
ROWS 11–20: Rep rows 3–4,
5 times.
Rep rows 9–20 twice more.
Rep rows 9–14 once more.
NEXT ROW (RS) (DEC): (K1, P1) twice,
[K1, (K2tog) 3 times, (K1, P1)
twice] 4 times, K1 (37 sts).
(51 rows)
Bind (cast) off sts.

⑥⑤ Triangle

SIZE

7in × 7in (18cm × 18cm)

MATERIALS

1 pair US 6 (4.00mm/No. 8)
  needles

⑥⑤ª First colorway (× 2⊞ ▣)

Rowan All Seasons Cotton
1¾oz (50g) balls

☐ green (A)		⅓
▨ blue (B)		⅛

☐ K on RS, P on WS

⑥⑤ᵇ Second colorway (× 2▣)

Rowan All Seasons Cotton
1¾oz (50g) balls

yellow (A)		⅓
blue (B)		⅛

KNIT

Cast on 37 sts and work until
chart row 49 completed.
Bind (cast) off sts.

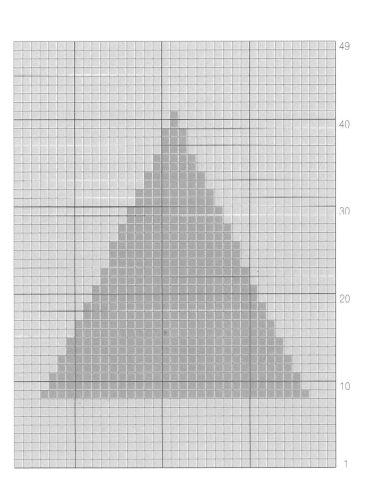

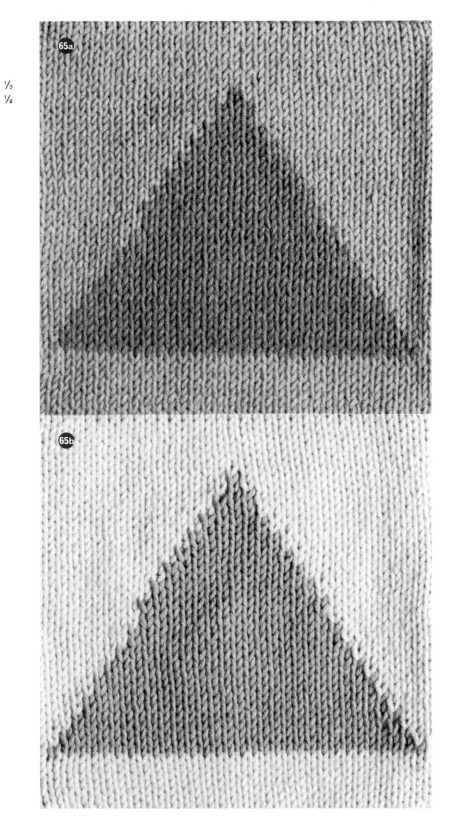

⑥⑥ Circle

SIZE
7in × 7in (18cm × 18cm)

MATERIALS
1 pair US 6 (4.00mm/No. 8)
   needles

⑥⑥ₐ First colorway (× 2⊞ ▣)
Rowan All Seasons Cotton
1³⁄₄oz (50g) balls
⬜ green (A)   ⅓
⬛ dark pink (B)   ⅙

☐ K on RS, P on WS

⑥⑥ᵦ Second colorway (× 2▣)
Rowan All Seasons Cotton
1³⁄₄oz (50g) balls
   yellow (A)   ⅓
   pale pink (B)   ⅙

KNIT
Cast on 37 sts and work until
chart row 50 completed.
Bind (cast) off sts.

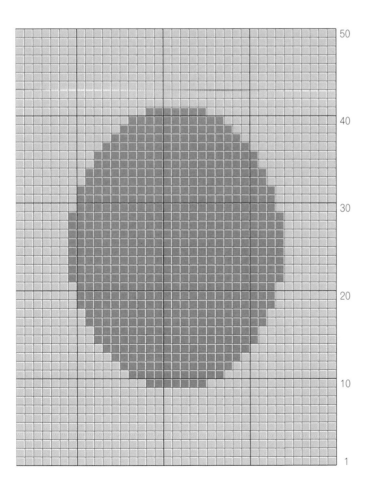

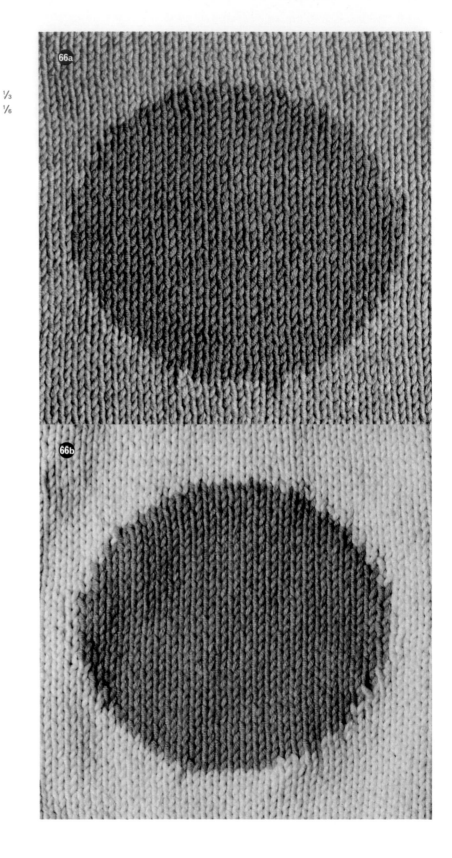

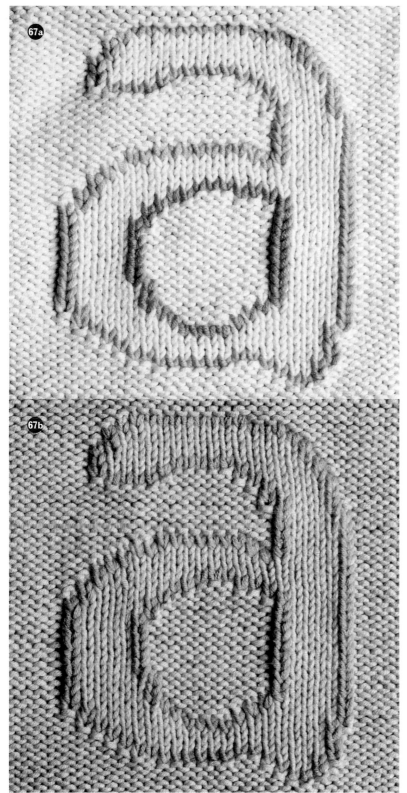

❻❼ The letter a

SIZE

7in × 7in (18cm × 18cm)

MATERIALS

1 pair US 6 (4.00mm/No. 8)
needles

❻❼ₐ First colorway (× 1⊞ ■)

Rowan All Seasons Cotton
1¾oz (50g) balls

☐ yellow (A)	½
■ blue (B)	⅟₂₅

☐ K on RS, P on WS
⊟ P on RS, K on WS

❻❼♭ Second colorway (× 1■)

Rowan All Seasons Cotton
1¾oz (50g) balls

green (A)	½
dark pink (B)	⅟₂₅

KNIT

Cast on 37 sts and work until
chart row 49 completed.
Bind (cast) off sts.

⑥⑧ The letter e

SIZE

7in × 7in (18cm × 18cm)

MATERIALS

1 pair US 6 (4.00mm/No. 8)
  needles

Single colorway (× 1 ⊞ ■)

Rowan All Seasons Cotton
1¾oz (50g) balls
□ green (A)   ½
■ dark pink (B)   ½₂₅

☐ K on RS, P on WS
⊟ P on RS, K on WS

KNIT

Cast on 38 sts and work until
chart row 50 completed.
Bind (cast) off sts.

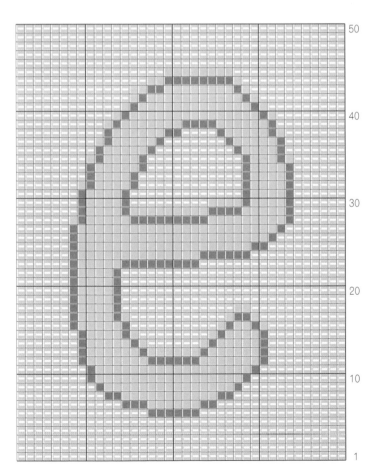

⑥⑨ The letter c

SIZE

7in × 7in (18cm × 18cm)

MATERIALS

1 pair US 6 (4.00mm/No. 8)
  needles

⑥⑨ₐ First colorway (× 1 ⊞ ■)

Rowan All Seasons Cotton
1¾oz (50g) balls
□ green (A)   ½
■ dark pink (B)   ½₂₅

☐ K on RS, P on WS
⊟ P on RS, K on WS

⑥⑨_b Second colorway (× 1 ■)

Rowan All Seasons Cotton
1¾oz (50g) balls
  yellow (A)   ½
  blue (B)   ½₂₅

KNIT

Cast on 37 sts and work until
chart row 49 completed.
Bind (cast) off sts.

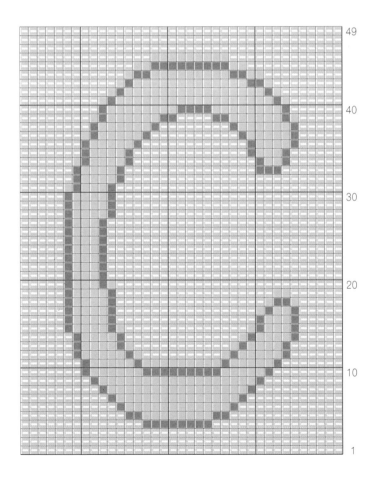

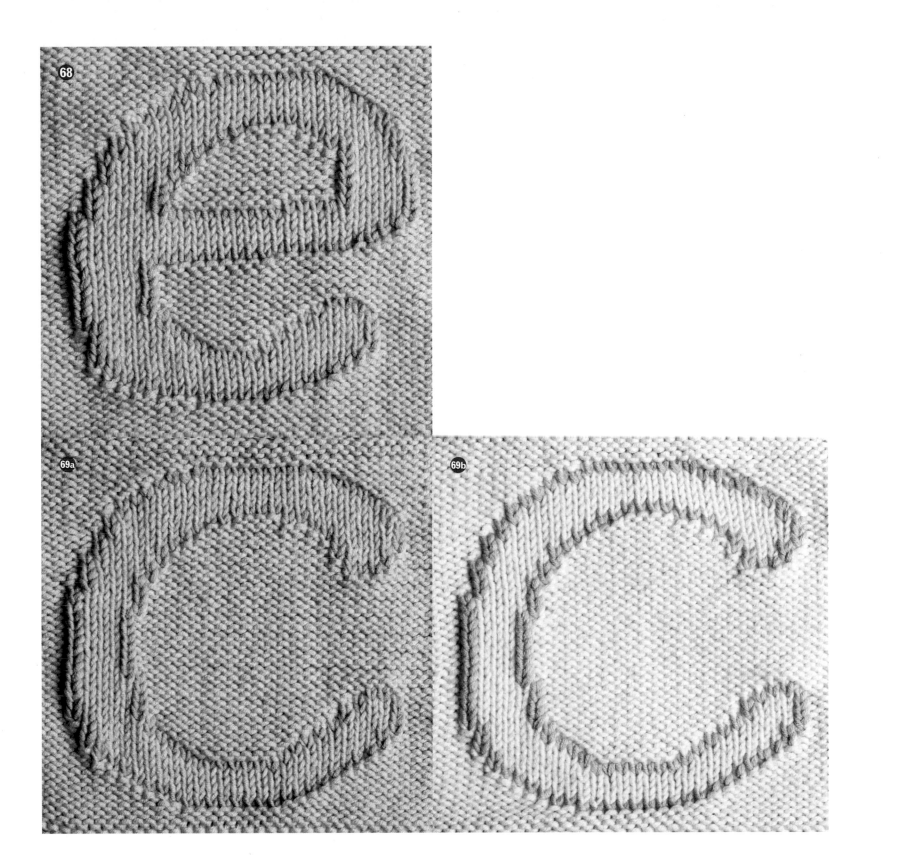

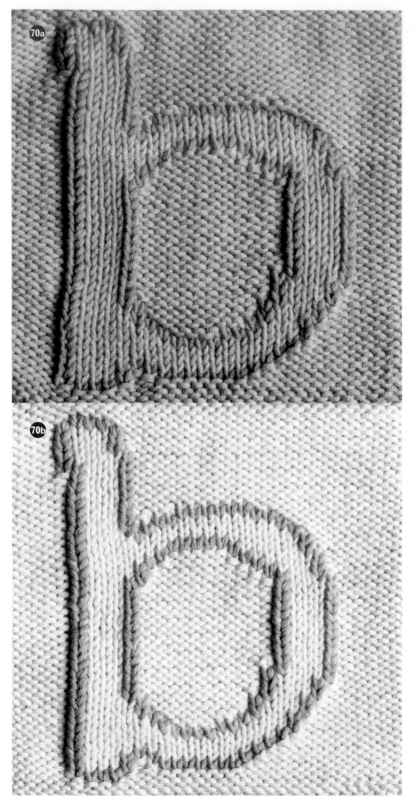

❼⓿ The letter b

SIZE
7in × 7in (18cm × 18cm)

MATERIALS
1 pair US 6 (4.00mm/No. 8) needles

⑦⓪ⓐ First colorway (× 1 ▦ ▣)
Rowan All Seasons Cotton
1³⁄₄oz (50g) balls
☐ green (A)   ¹⁄₂
▨ dark pink (B)   ¹⁄₂

☐ K on RS, P on WS
⊟ P on RS, K on WS

⑦⓪ⓑ Second colorway (× 1 ▣)
Rowan All Seasons Cotton
1³⁄₄oz (50g) balls
   yellow (A)   ¹⁄₂
   blue (B)   ¹⁄₂₅

KNIT
Cast on 37 sts and work until chart row 50 completed. Bind (cast) off sts.

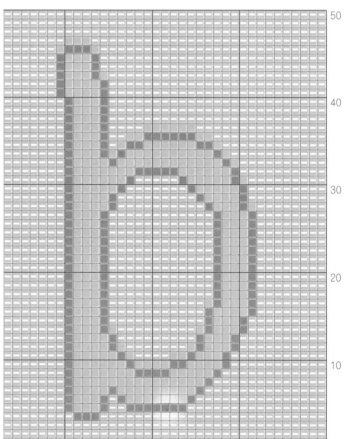

The letter f

SIZE
7in × 7in (18cm × 18cm)

MATERIALS
1 pair US 6 (4.00mm/No. 8)
  needles

Single colorway (× 1 ⊞ ◼)
Rowan All Seasons Cotton
1¾oz (50g) balls
☐ yellow (A)   ½
◻ blue (B)   ¹/₂₅

☐ K on RS, P on WS
⊟ P on RS, K on WS

KNIT
Cast on 37 sts and work until
chart row 50 completed.
Bind (cast) off sts.

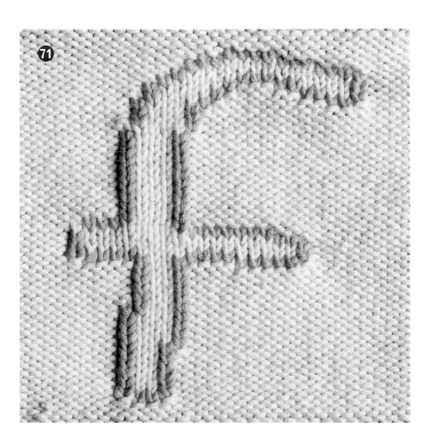

retro

In the inter-related world of fashion and music, the Sixties, Seventies, and Eighties are constantly revisited to provide inspiration for today's designers and musicians. I am aware that contemporary design trends often borrow influences from those dynamic years and for this design I have chosen to focus on the Seventies. This is the period in which I grew up and I remember it well as being bright, colorful, and very inspirational. The Retro afghan combines Fair Isle tank-top stripe patterns and Seventies' graphics in a subtle palette of colors to bring the spirit of the flamboyant decade into present-day living.

SIZE
66in × 54in (165cm × 135cm)

MATERIALS
1 pair US 2–3 (3.00mm/No. 11)
    needles
2 circular US 2 (2.75mm/No. 12)
    needles 32in (80cm) length
Cable needle

Yarn
Rowan Cotton Glace
1¾oz (50g) balls

mid yellow	12
mid blue	12
chocolate	11
light beige	5

Quantities given for individual squares are approximate fractions of a ball.

GAUGE (TENSION)
25 sts and 34 rows to 4in (10cm) measured over stockinette (stocking) stitch using US 2–3 (3.00mm/No. 11) needles.

NOTE
Single stitch outlines on squares 72a, 72b, 73a, 73b, 75a and 75b can be Swiss-darned after knitting (see page 122).

ABBREVIATIONS
See page 127.

FINISHING
The sizes given for the finished afghan and individual squares are approximate. The number of stitches in a row, and the number of rows in a square differ in some instances. Therefore, when sewing pieces together, ease the extra stitches or rows into the adjoining square.

    Press the individual squares using a damp cloth and a warm iron. Sew the squares together, joining bound (cast) off edge of one square to the cast-on edge of the next square, easing in stitches, if necessary, to form vertical strips. Sew the vertical strips together, easing in rows, if necessary, to create one block.

Edging

MATERIALS

2 circular US 2 (2.75mm/No. 12) needles 32in (80cm) length

Yarn

Rowan Cotton Glace
1¾oz (50g) balls

mid blue	2

KNIT

With RS facing, pick up and knit 411 sts along the RH edge of the afghan.
Beg with a WS row, work 6 rows in garter stitch (knit every row), inc 1 st at each end of the WS rows (417 sts).
Bind (cast) off sts knitwise
Rep for LH edge of the afghan.
With RS facing, pick up and knit 325 sts along bottom edge of the afghan. Rep edging as for RH and LH edges.
Rep for top edge of afghan.
Neatly sew border edges together.

Order of squares

72a	72b	72a	72b	72a	72b	72a	72b	72a
72b	73a	76	75a	77	73a	76	75a	72b
72a	74b	75b	74a	73b	74b	75b	74a	72a
72b	75a	77	73a	76	75a	77	73a	72b
72a	74a	73b	74b	75b	74a	73b	74b	72a
72b	73a	76	75a	77	73a	76	75a	72b
72a	74b	75b	74a	73b	74b	75b	74a	72a
72b	75a	77	73a	76	75a	77	73a	72b
72a	74a	73b	74b	75b	74a	73b	74b	72a
72b	73a	76	75a	77	73a	76	75a	72b
72a	72b	72a	72b	72a	72b	72a	72b	72a

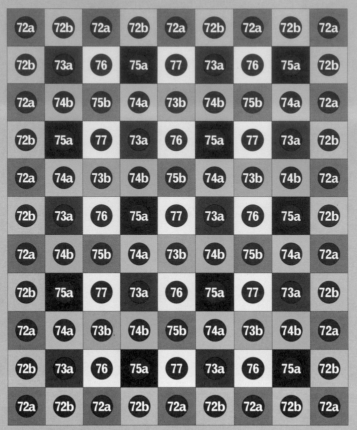

QUANTITY OF SQUARES

(72) Retro square	
(72a) First colorway	18
(72b) Second colorway	18
(73) Lozenge	
(73a) First colorway	10
(73b) Second colorway	6
(74) Tank-top stripe	
(74a) First colorway	8
(74b) Second colorway	8
(75) Lozenge II	
(75a) First colorway	10
(75b) Second colorway	6
(76) Fab stripe	8
(77) Groovy cable	7

(72) Retro square

SIZE

6in × 6in (15cm × 15cm)

MATERIALS

1 pair US 2–3 (3.00mm/No. 11) needles

(72a) First colorway (× 18)

Rowan Cotton Glace
1¾oz (50g) balls

■ chocolate (A)	1/6
□ mid yellow (B)	1/10
■ mid blue (C)	1/25
□ light beige (D)	1/50

□ K on RS, P on WS

(72b) Second colorway (× 18)

Rowan Cotton Glace
1¾oz (50g) balls

mid yellow (A)	1/6
mid blue (B)	1/10
chocolate (C)	1/25
light beige (D)	1/50

KNIT

Cast on 37 sts using A and work until chart row 50 completed.
Bind (cast) off sts.

72a

72b

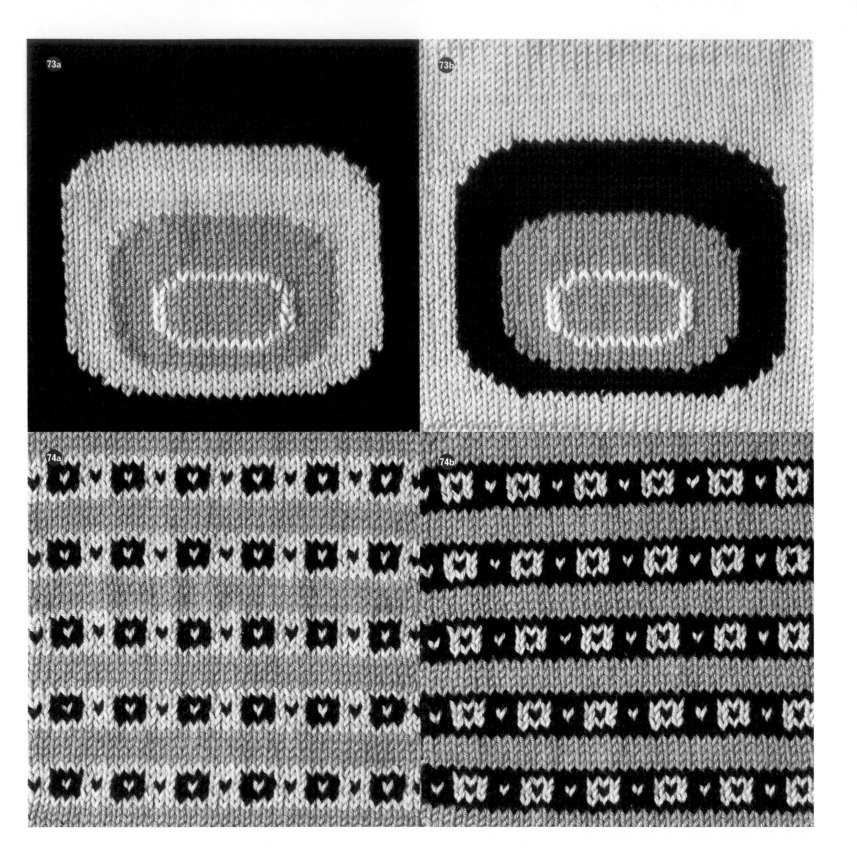

❼❸ Lozenge

SIZE
6in × 6in (15cm × 15cm)

MATERIALS
1 pair US 2–3 (3.00mm/No. 11)
    needles

❼❸ₐ First colorway (× 10⊞ ▣)
Rowan Cotton Glace
1³⁄₄oz (50g) balls
- ■ chocolate (A) ⅙
- ☐ mid yellow (B) ¹⁄₁₀
- ■ mid blue (C) ¹⁄₁₆
- ☐ light beige (D) ¹⁄₅₀

☐ K on RS, P on WS

❼❸ᵦ Second colorway (× 6▣)
Rowan Cotton Glace
1³⁄₄oz (50g) balls
- mid yellow (A) ⅙
- chocolate (B) ¹⁄₁₀
- mid blue (C) ¹⁄₁₀
- light beige (D) ¹⁄₅₀

KNIT
Cast on 38 sts and work until
chart row 50 completed.
Bind (cast) off sts.

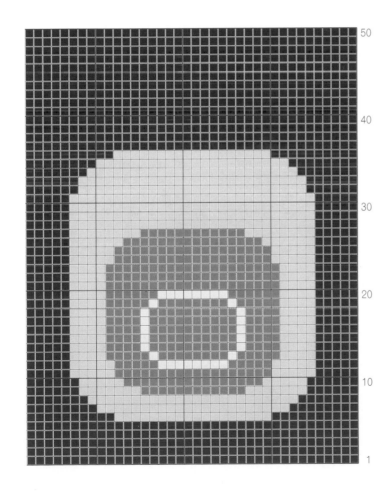

❼❹ Tank-top stripe

SIZE
6in × 6in (15cm × 15cm)

MATERIALS
1 pair US 2–3 (3.00mm/No. 11)
    needles

❼❹ₐ First colorway (× 8▣)
Rowan Cotton Glace
1³⁄₄oz (50g) balls
- mid blue (A) ⅟₇
- mid yellow (B) ⅛
- chocolate (C) ¹⁄₁₆

❼❹ᵦ Second colorway (× 8▣)
Rowan Cotton Glace
1³⁄₄oz (50g) balls
- mid blue (A) ⅟₇
- chocolate (B) ⅛
- mid yellow (C) ¹⁄₁₆

KNIT
Cast on 39 sts using A.
Working in stockinette (stocking)
stitch, cont in stripe patt rep as
folls, beg with a RS row:
*ROWS 1–4: A.
ROW 5 (RS): B.
ROW 6 (WS): (P3B, P3C) 6 times,
P3B.
ROW 7 (RS): (K1B, K1C) 19 times,
K1B.
ROW 8 (WS): (P3B, P3C) 6 times,
P3B.
ROW 9 (RS): B.
Transfer stitches back onto LH
needle, so that RS is facing
again.*
Rep from * to * 4 more times.
ROWS 46–49: A.
(49 rows)
Bind (cast) off sts.

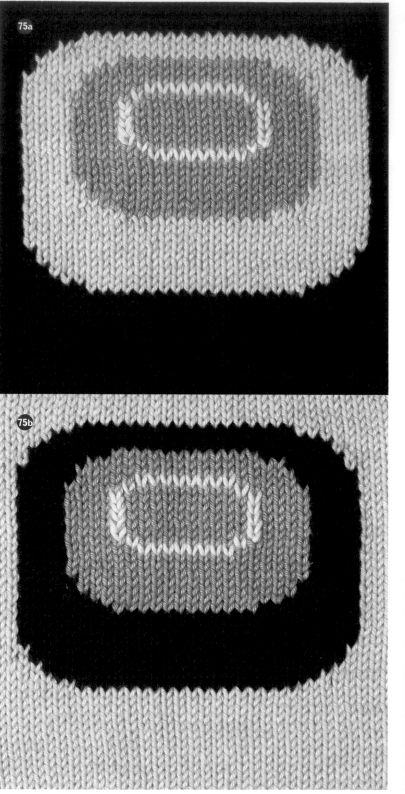

⑦⑤ Lozenge II

SIZE

6in × 6in (15cm × 15cm)

MATERIALS

1 pair US 2–3 (3.00mm/No. 11)
   needles

⑦⑤ᵃ First colorway (× 10⊞ ▣)

Rowan Cotton Glace
1¾oz (50g) balls

■	chocolate (A)	⅙
▢	mid yellow (B)	¹⁄₁₀
■	mid blue (C)	¹⁄₁₆
▢	light beige (D)	¹⁄₅₀

▢ K on RS, P on WS

⑦⑤ᵇ Second colorway (× 6▣)

Rowan Cotton Glace
1¾oz (50g) balls

mid yellow (A)	⅙
chocolate (B)	¹⁄₁₀
mid blue (C)	¹⁄₁₆
light beige (D)	¹⁄₅₀

KNIT

Cast on 38 sts and work until
chart row 50 completed.
Bind (cast) off sts.

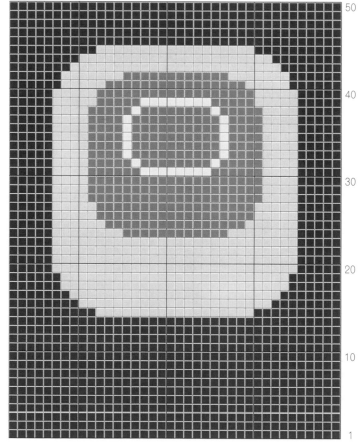

⓻ Fab stripe

SIZE
6in × 6in (15cm × 15cm)

MATERIALS
1 pair US 2–3 (3.00mm/No. 11)
   needles

Single colorway (× 8▣)
Rowan Cotton Glace
1³/₄oz (50g) balls
   light beige (A)   ⅛
   mid blue (B)   ¹/₁₂
   mid yellow (C)   ¹/₁₂
   chocolate (D)   ¹/₁₆

KNIT
Cast on 38 sts using A.
Working in stockinette (stocking)
stitch (K on RS rows, P on WS
rows), cont in stripe patt rep as
folls, beg with a RS row:
ROWS 1–4: **A.**
ROWS 5–8: **B.**
ROWS 9–12: **C.**
ROWS 13–17: **D.**
ROWS 18–21: **A.**
ROWS 22–25: **C.**
ROWS 26–29: **B.**
ROWS 30–33: **A.**
ROWS 34–38: **D.**
ROWS 39–42: **C.**
ROWS 43–46: **B.**
ROWS 47–50: **A.**
Bind (cast) off sts.

⓽ Groovy cable

SIZE
6in × 6in (15cm × 15cm)

MATERIALS
1 pair US 2–3 (3.00mm/No. 11)
   needles
Cable needle

Single colorway (× 7▣)
Rowan Cotton Glace
1³/₄oz (50g) balls
   light beige (A)   ⅕
   mid blue (B)   ⅓
   mid yellow (C)   small amount
   chocolate (D)   small amount

KNIT
Cast on 38 sts in the foll
sequence: (3A, 4B) 5 times, 3A.
ROW 1 (RS) (INC): **P3A, (B inc once
into each of the next 4 sts, P3A)
5 times (58 sts).**
ROW 2 (WS): **K3A, (P8B, K3A)
5 times.**
ROW 3 (RS): **P3A, (c8bB, P3A)
5 times.**
ROW 4 (WS): **Rep row 2.**
ROW 5 (RS): **P3A, (K8B, P3A)
5 times.**
ROW 6–13: **Rep rows 4–5, 4 times.**
ROW 14 (WS): **As row 4.**
Rep rows 3–14, 3 times more.
Rep row 3 once more.
NEXT ROW (WS) (DEC): **K3A, (P2togB
4 times, K3A) 5 times
(38 sts).**
(52 rows)
Bind (cast) off sts.

Using the photograph as a guide,
Swiss-darn small blocks of 4 sts
onto knitting using A, C and D.

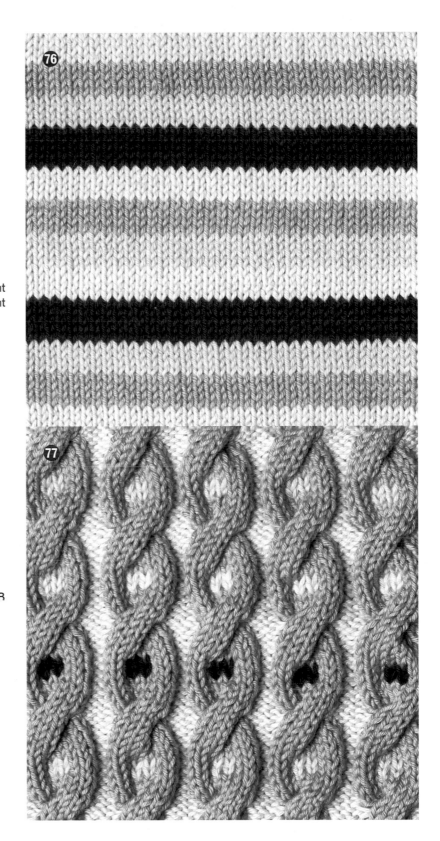

sherbert dips & candy twists

The colorful sweets and treats found in your local candy store were the inspiration for this afghan. At first glance, this design appears to be quite complex and busy. However, a closer examination will reveal that the whole design comprises of just five different squares knitted in cables and simple stripe patterns, with buttons sewn on for extra decoration. This afghan would be a welcome addition to any child's bedroom or play area, adding a cheery splash of color.

SIZE

85in × 59in (213cm × 148cm)

MATERIALS

1 pair US 5 (3.75mm/No. 9) needles
2 circular US 2–3 (3.00mm/No. 11) needles 32in (80cm) length
Cable needle

Yarn

Rowan Handknit DK Cotton
1³⁄₄oz (50g) balls

yellow	7
lilac	11
green	15
orange	12
pink	13

Quantities given for individual squares are approximate fractions of a ball

Buttons

shell	360

GAUGE (TENSION)

22 sts and 30 rows to 4in (10cm) measured over stockinette (stocking) stitch using US 5 (3.75mm/No. 9) needles.

ABBREVIATIONS

See page 127.

FINISHING

The sizes given for the finished afghan and individual squares are approximate. The number of stitches in a row, and the number of rows in a square differ in some instances. Therefore, when sewing pieces together, ease the extra stitches or rows into the adjoining square.

Press the individual squares using a damp cloth and a warm iron. Sew the squares together, joining bound- (cast-) off edge of one square to the cast-on edge of the next square, easing in stitches, if necessary, to form vertical strips. Sew the vertical strips together, easing in rows, if necessary, to create one block.

Edging

MATERIALS

2 circular US 2–3 (3.00mm/No.11)
  needles 32in (80cm) length

Yarn

Rowan Handknit DK Cotton
1¾oz (50g) balls
  yellow (A)   ⁴/₅
  pink (B)   ⁴/₅
  green (C)   ⁴/₅
  lilac (D)   ⁴/₅

KNIT

With RS facing and using A, pick
up and knit 491 sts along the RH
edge of the afghan.
Beg with a WS row, work 5 rows
in garter stitch (knit every row), inc
one st at each end of the WS rows
(497 sts).
Push sts to other end of the
circular needle so that the WS is
facing again.
Bind (cast) off sts knitwise.
Rep for LH edge of afghan using B.
With RS facing and C, pick up and
knit 327 sts along bottom edge of
the afghan.
Rep edging as for RH and LH
edges.
Rep for top edge of afghan using D.
Neatly sew border edges together.

Order of squares

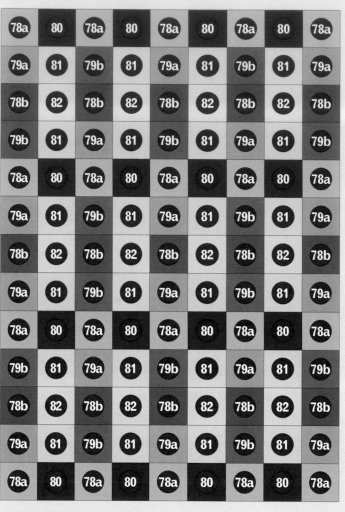

QUANTITY OF SQUARES

78 Refresher
  78a First colorway   20
  78b Second colorway   15
79 Sweeties
  79a First colorway   16
  79b Second colorway   14
80 Candy twist 1   16
81 Sherbert stripe   24
82 Candy twist 2   12

78 Refresher

SIZE

6½in × 6½in (16.5cm × 16.5cm)

MATERIALS

1 pair US 5 (3.75mm/No. 9)
  needles

78a **First colorway** (× 20 ▣)
Rowan Handknit DK Cotton
1¾oz (50g) balls
  yellow (A)   ⅛
  green (B)   ⅟₇
  lilac (C)   ⅟₇

78b **Second colorway** (× 15)
Rowan Handknit DK Cotton
1¾oz (50g) balls
  yellow (A)   ⅛
  pink (B)   ⅟₇
  orange (C)   ⅟₇

KNIT

Cast on 38 sts using A.
Note: Do not cut off yarns. Carry
them up the side of the work.
Working in stockinette (stocking)
stitch (knit on RS rows and purl on
WS rows), and beg with a RS row,
cont in stripe patt rep as folls:
ROWS 1–2: **A.**
ROWS 3–5: **B.**
ROWS 6–8: **C.**
ROWS 9–10: **A.**
ROWS 11–13: **C.**
ROWS 14–16: **B.**
Rep rows 1–16 twice more.
Rep rows 1–2 once more.
(50 rows)
Bind (cast) off sts.

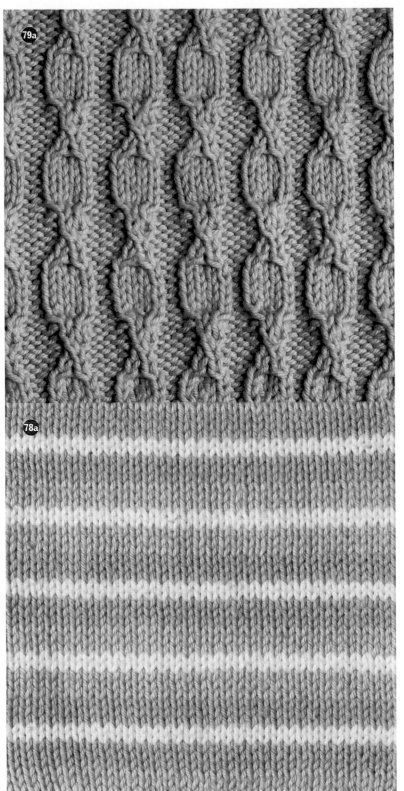

㊐ Sweeties

SIZE

6½in × 6½in (16.5cm × 16.5cm)

MATERIALS

1 pair US 5 (3.75mm/No. 9)
   needles
Cable needle

㊆ First colorway (× 16▣)

Rowan Handknit DK Cotton
1¾oz (50g) balls
   lilac   ½

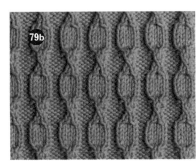

㊆ Second colorway (× 14▣)

Rowan Cotton Glace
1¾oz (50g) balls
   orange   ½

KNIT

Cast on 37 sts.

ROW 1 (RS) (INC): P2, (K1, inc once into next st, K1, P2) 7 times (44 sts).

ROW 2 (WS): K2, (P4, K2) 7 times.

ROW 3 (RS): P2, (K4, P2) 7 times.

ROW 4 (WS): As row 2.

ROW 5 (RS): P2, (sl next st onto cable needle and hold at front of work, P1, then K1 from cable needle, sl next st onto cable needle and hold at back of work, K1, then P1 from cable needle, P2) 7 times.

ROW 6 (WS): K3, (P2, K4) 6 times, P2, K3.

ROW 7 (RS): P3, (K2, P4) 6 times, K2, P3.

ROW 8 (WS): K3, (sl next st onto cable needle and hold at front of work facing towards you, P1, then P1 from cable needle, K3) 6 times, sl next st onto cable needle and hold at front of work facing towards you, P1, then P1 from cable needle, K3.

ROW 9 (RS): As row 7.

ROW 10 (WS): As row 6.

ROW 11 (RS): P2, (sl next st onto cable needle and hold at back of work, K1, then K1 from cable needle, sl next st onto cable needle and hold at front of work, K1, K1 from cable needle, P2) 7 times.

ROW 12 (WS): As row 2.

ROWS 13–16: Rep rows 3–4 twice.

Rep rows 5–16 twice more.

Rep rows 5–13 once more.

NEXT ROW (WS) (DEC): K2, (P1, P2tog, P1, K2) 7 times (37 sts).
(50 rows)

Bind (cast) off sts.

⑧⓪ Candy twist 1

SIZE
6½in × 6½in (16.5cm × 16.5cm)

MATERIALS
1 pair US 5 (3.75mm/No. 9)
   needles
Cable needle

Single colorway (× 16■)
Rowan Handknit DK Cotton
1¾oz (50g) balls
   pink   ½

KNIT
Cast on 38 sts.
ROW 1 (RS) (INC): P3, (K1, inc once
into each of next 2 sts, K1, P3) 5
times (48 sts).
ROW 2 (WS): K3, (P6, K3) 5 times.
ROW 3 (RS): P3, (K6, P3) 5 times.
ROW 4 (WS): As row 2.

ROWS 5–8: Rep rows 3–4
twice.
ROW 9 (RS): P3, (sl next 2 sts onto
cable needle and hold at front of
work, K4, then K2 from cable
needle, P3) 5 times.
ROW 10 (WS): As row 2.
ROWS 11–20: Rep rows 3–4, 5
times.
ROW 21 (RS): P3, (sl next 4 sts onto
cable needle and hold at back of
work, K2, then K4 from cable
needle, P3) 5 times.
ROW 22 (WS): As row 2.
ROWS 23–32: Rep rows 3–4, 5
times.
Rep rows 9–26 once more.
NEXT ROW (RS) (DEC): P3, [K1,
(K2tog) twice, K1, P3] 5 times
(38 sts).
(51 rows)
Bind (cast) off sts.

⑧① Sherbert stripe

SIZE
6½in × 6½in (16.5cm × 16.5cm)

MATERIALS
1 pair US 5 (3.75mm/No. 9)
   needles

Single colorway (× 24■)
Rowan Handknit DK Cotton
1¾oz (50g) balls
   yellow (A)   ¹⁄₁₂
   green (B)   ¹⁄₆
   pink (C)   ¹⁄₁₀
   orange (D)   ¹⁄₁₂
   lilac (E)   ¹⁄₅₀

Buttons
   shell   15

KNIT
Cast on 37 sts.
ROW 1 (RS): A, knit.
ROW 2 (WS): A, purl.
ROW 3 (RS): K1B, (P1B, K1B) 18
times.
ROW 4 (WS): B, purl.
ROW 5 (RS): D, knit.
ROW 6 (WS): D, purl.
ROW 7 (RS): B, knit.
ROW 8 (WS): B, purl.
ROW 9 (RS): C, knit.
ROW 10 (WS): C, purl.
ROWS 11–12: Rep rows 7–8.
ROWS 13–14: Rep rows 5–6.
ROWS 15–16: Rep rows 7–8.
ROW 17 (RS): K1A, (P1A, K1A) 18
times.
ROW 18 (WS): A, purl.
ROW 19 (RS): C, knit.
ROW 20 (WS): C, purl.
ROW 21 (RS): E, knit.
ROW 22 (WS): E, purl.

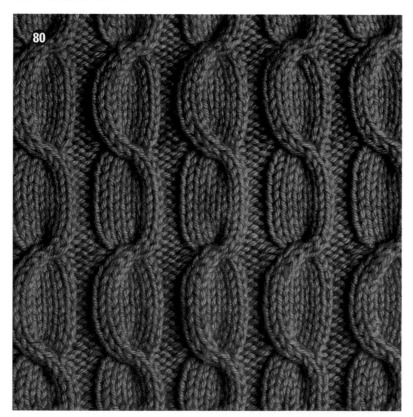

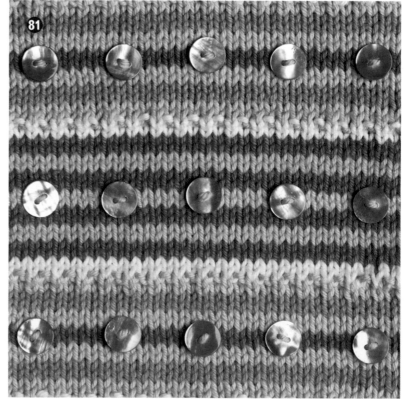

ROWS 23–24: **Rep rows 19–20.**
ROW 25 (RS): **B, knit.**
ROW 26 (WS): **B, purl.**
ROWS 27–32: **Rep rows 19–24.**
ROWS 33–34: **Rep rows 1–2.**
ROWS 35 48: **Rep rows 3–16.**
ROWS 49–50: **Rep rows 17–18.**
Bind (cast) off sts.

Using the photograph as a guide, sew buttons onto stripes.

❽❷ Candy twist 2

SIZE
6½in × 6½in (16.5cm × 16.5cm)

MATERIALS
1 pair US 5 (3.75mm/No. 9)
  needles
Cable needle

Single colorway (× 12◼)
Rowan Cotton Glace
1¾oz (50g) balls
  green   ½

KNIT
Cast on 38 sts.
ROW 1 (RS) (INC): **P3, (K1, inc once into each of next 2 sts, K1, P3) 5 times (48 sts).**
ROW 2 (WS): **K3, (P6, K3) 5 times.**
ROW 3 (RS): **P3, (K6, P3) 5 times.**
ROW 4 (WS): **As row 2.**
ROWS 5–8: **Rep rows 3–4 twice.**
ROW 9 (RS): **P3, (sl next 4 sts onto cable needle and hold at back of work, K2, then K4 sts from cable needle, P3) 5 times.**
ROW 10 (WS): **As row 2.**

ROWS 11–20: **Rep rows 3–4, 5 times.**
ROW 21 (RS): **P3, (sl next 2 sts onto cable needle and hold at front of work, K4, then K2 sts from cable needle, P3) 5 times.**
ROW 22 (WS): **As row 2.**
ROWS 23–32: **Rep rows 3–4, 5 times.**
Rep rows 9–26 once more.
NEXT ROW (RS) (DEC): **P3, [K1, (K2tog) twice, K1, P3] 5 times (38 sts).**
(51 rows)
Bind (cast) off sts.

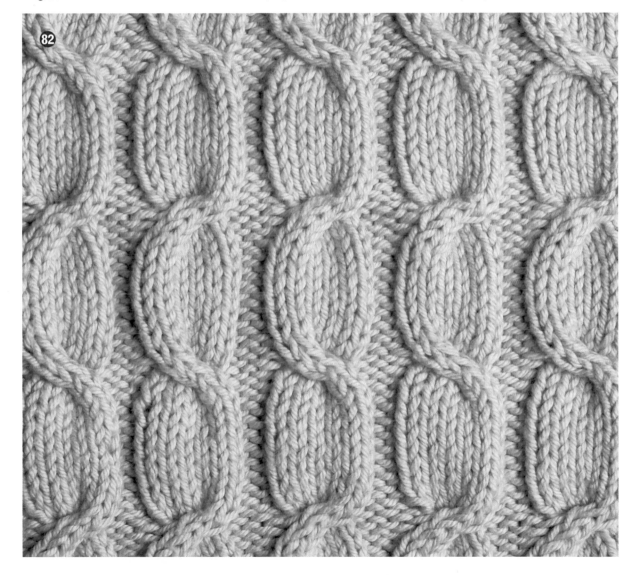

the circus

Bring on the clowns! In this design I have indulged my love of circuses, recollecting the colorful images I saw as a child. The big top housed a captivating spectacle, vibrant and full of color and movement. I have included the popular and familiar images of the sad and happy clowns, and the magic of the circus is suggested by the sparkling black and silver beaded Magic Curtain. This afghan would add a touch of razzmatazz to a young person's den, with its evocation of childhood delights. Roll up, roll up, pick up your knitting needles and join in the fun of the circus!

SIZE
54in × 42in (135cm × 105cm)

MATERIALS
1 pair US 5 (3.75mm/No. 9)
    needles
2 circular US 2–3 (3.00mm/No. 11)
    needles 32in (80cm) length
Cable needle

Yarn
Rowan Wool Cotton
1¾oz (50g) balls

aqua	4
royal blue	4
yellow	3
black	7
red	3
cream	2
navy blue	4
pink	3
purple	3

Rowan Kidsilk Haze
(Used triple throughout)
1oz (25g) balls

bright pink	1

(Used triple throughout)

Quantities given for individual squares are approximate fractions of a ball.

Beads
⅛in (3mm) beads

silver	3280
blue	1891

³⁄₁₆in (5mm) beads

red	112

GAUGE (TENSION)
24 sts and 32 rows to 4in (10cm) measured over stockinette (stocking) stitch using US 5 (3.75mm/No. 9) needles.

NOTE
Single stitch outlines on squares ⑧③, ⑧⑤, ⑧⑥, ⑧⑧ and ⑨⓪ can be Swiss-darned after knitting (see page 122).

ABBREVIATIONS
See page 127.

FINISHING
The sizes given for the finished afghan and individual squares are approximate. The number of stitches in a row, and the number of rows in a square differ in some instances. Therefore, when sewing pieces together, ease the extra stitches or rows into the adjoining square.

Press the individual squares using a damp cloth and a warm iron. Sew the squares together, joining bound (cast) off edge of one square to the cast-on edge of the next square, easing in stitches, if necessary, to form vertical strips. Sew the vertical strips together, easing in rows, if necessary, to create one block.

Edging

MATERIALS
2 circular US 2–3 (3.00mm/No. 11) needles 32in (80cm) length

Yarn
Rowan Wool Cotton
1¾oz (50g) balls

purple (A)	³⁄₅
black (B)	⁴⁄₅
green (C)	⁴⁄₅
yellow (D)	½
red (E)	½

KNIT
With RS facing and using A, pick up and knit 335 sts along the RH edge of the afghan.
Beg with a WS row, cont to work in garter stitch (knit every row) for 5 rows, inc 1 st at each end of all RS rows.
NEXT ROW (RS): B, inc once into first st, P to last 2 sts, inc once into next st, P1 (341 sts).
NEXT ROW (WS): B, knit.
NEXT ROW (RS): B, inc once into first st, K to last 2 sts, inc once into next st, K1 (343 sts).
With WS facing bind (cast) off sts knitwise.
Rep for LH edge of afghan, using C in place of A.
With RS facing and using D, pick up and knit 247 sts along bottom edge of the afghan.

Rep edging as for RH edge, using D in place of A.
Rep for top edge of afghan, using E in place of D.

Order of squares

83	88a	90	88b	86	88a	83
84	89a	84	89b	84	89a	84
87	88b	85	88a	87	88b	85
84	89a	84	89b	84	89a	84
86	88a	83	88b	83	88a	90
84	89a	84	89b	84	89a	84
85	88b	87	88a	85	88b	87
84	89a	84	89b	84	89a	84
83	88a	90	88b	86	88a	83

QUANTITY OF SQUARES

83	Big top	6
84	Magic curtain	16
85	Balloons	4
86	Happy clown	3
87	Circus ball	4
88	Spangles and stars	
88a	First colorway	8
88b	Second colorway	7
89	Streamers	
89a	First colorway	8
89b	Second colorway	4
90	Sad clown	3

83 Big top

SIZE
6in × 6in (15cm x 15cm)

MATERIALS
1 pair US 5 (3.75mm/No. 9) needles
Single colorway (× 6 ▦ ▣)
Rowan Wool Cotton
1¾oz (50g) balls

▨	aqua	¼
▨	royal blue	¹⁄₁₆
■	black	¹⁄₂₅
▨	red	¹⁄₂₅
☐	cream	¹⁄₂₅
☐	yellow	¹⁄₅₀

☐ K on RS, P on WS

KNIT
Cast on 38 sts and work until chart row 50 completed.
Bind (cast) off sts.

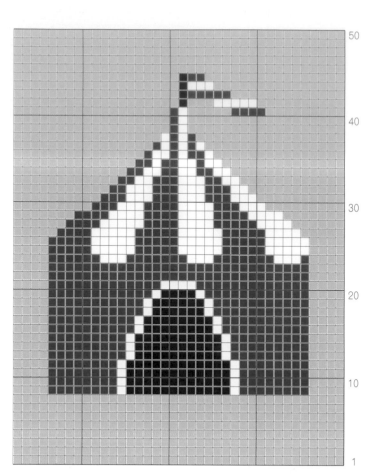

83

84 Magic curtain

SIZE
6in × 6in (15cm × 15cm)

MATERIALS
1 pair US 5 (3.75mm/No. 9)
  needles

Single colorway (× 16■)
Rowan Wool Cotton
1¾oz (50g) balls
  black ⅓

⅛in (3mm) beads
  silver 198

KNIT
Thread 198 silver beads onto yarn.
Cast on 37 sts.
ROW 1 (RS): Knit.
ROW 2 (WS): Purl.
ROW 3 (RS): Knit.
ROW 4 (WS): Purl.
ROW 5 (RS): K2, (pb, K3) 8 times,
pb, K2.
ROW 6 (WS): Purl.
ROW 7 (RS): K3, (pb, K1) 15 times,
pb, K3.
ROW 8 (WS): Purl.
ROW 9 (RS): K4, (pb, K3) 8 times,
K1.
ROW 10 (WS): Purl.
Rep rows 3–10, 5 times more.
NEXT ROW (RS): Knit.
(51 rows)
Bind (cast) off sts.

85 Balloons

SIZE
6in × 6in (15cm × 15cm)

MATERIALS
1 pair US 5 (3.75mm/No. 9)
  needles

Single colorway (× 4⊞ ■)
Rowan Wool Cotton
1¾oz (50g) balls
☐ yellow ¼
■ purple ¹⁄₅₀
■ red ¹⁄₅₀
■ aqua ¹⁄₅₀
■ pink ¹⁄₅₀
■ green ¹⁄₅₀
■ royal blue ¹⁄₅₀
■ navy blue ¹⁄₅₀

☐ K on RS, P on WS

KNIT
Cast on 37 sts and work until
chart row 50 completed.
Bind (cast) off sts.

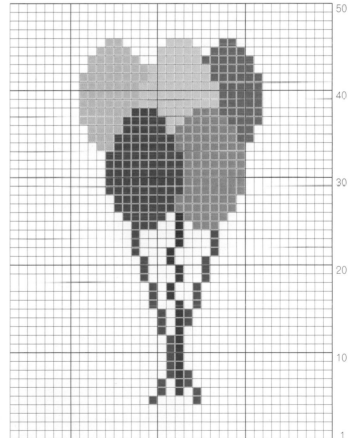

86 Happy clown

SIZE
6in × 6in (15cm × 15cm)

MATERIALS
1 pair US 5 (3.75mm/No. 9)
  needles

Single colorway (× 3 ▦ ▣)
Rowan Wool Cotton
1¾oz (50g) balls

■ pink (A)	¼
☐ cream (B)	¹⁄₁₆
■ black (C)	¹⁄₅₀
■ purple (D)	¹⁄₅₀
■ green (E)	¹⁄₅₀
☐ yellow (F)	¹⁄₁₂
■ red (G)	¹⁄₅₀

⅛in (3mm) beads
● blue   63

☐ K on RS, P on WS
◉ mb = make bobble (see page 123)

KNIT
Thread 30 blue beads onto A, and 33 blue beads onto F.
Cast on 37 sts and work until chart row 50 completed.
Bind (cast) off sts.

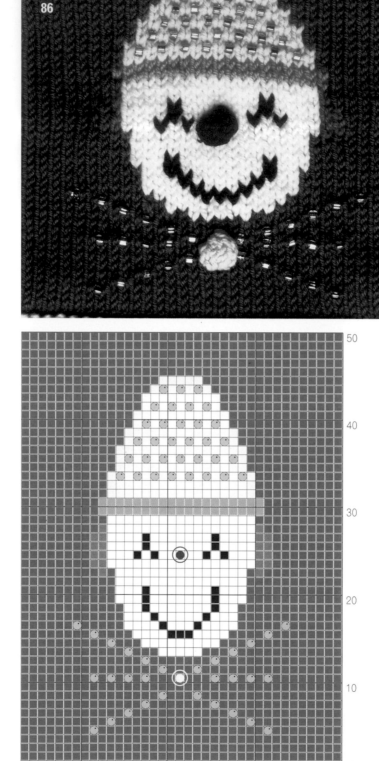

87 Circus ball

SIZE
6in × 6in (15cm × 15cm)

MATERIALS
1 pair US 5 (3.75mm/No. 9)
  needles

Single colorway (× 4 ▦ ▣)
Rowan Wool Cotton
1¾oz (50g) balls

■ red	¼
■ aqua	¹⁄₂₅
☐ yellow	¹⁄₂₅
■ royal blue	¹⁄₅₀

☐ K on RS, P on WS
✕ embroider cross

KNIT
Cast on 38 sts and work until chart row 50 completed.
Bind (cast) off sts.
Using the photograph as a guide, embroider crosses onto circus ball.

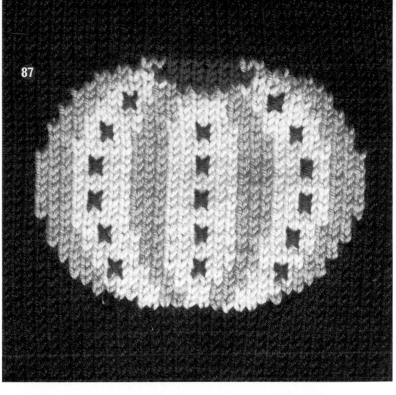

87

88 Spangles and stars

SIZE
6In × 6In (15cm × 15cm)

MATERIALS
1 pair US 5 (3.75mm/No. 9) needles

88a First colorway (× 8⊞ ▣)
Rowan Wool Cotton
1³⁄₄oz (50g) balls

■ royal blue (A)	¹⁄₃
■ red (B)	¹⁄₅₀
■ green (C)	¹⁄₅₀
□ yellow (D)	¹⁄₅₀

¹⁄₈in (3mm) beads
◐ blue	100
◔ silver	7

³⁄₁₆in (5mm) beads
● red	7

□ K on RS, P on WS

88b Second colorway (× 7▣)
Rowan Wool Cotton
1³⁄₄oz (50g) balls

navy blue (A)	¹⁄₃
red (B)	¹⁄₅₀
green (C)	¹⁄₅₀
yellow (D)	¹⁄₅₀

¹⁄₈in (3mm) beads
blue	100
silver	7

³⁄₁₆in (5mm) beads
red	7

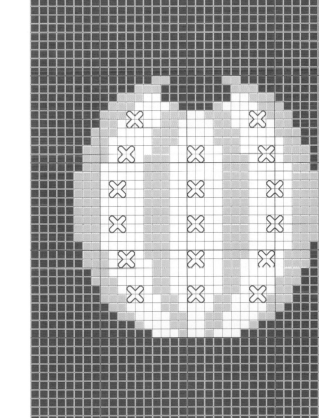

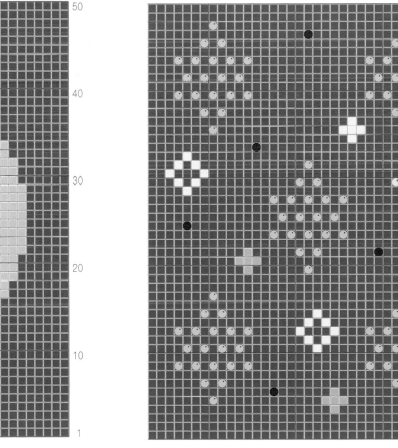

KNIT

Thread beads onto A in the foll sequence: 2 blue, 1 red, 36 blue, 1 red, 2 blue, 1 red, 2 silver, 1 blue, 3 silver, 2 blue, 2 silver, 9 blue, 1 red, 5 blue, 1 red, 41 blue, 1 red, 2 blue, 1 red.
Cast on 37 sts and work until chart row 50 completed.
Bind (cast) off sts.

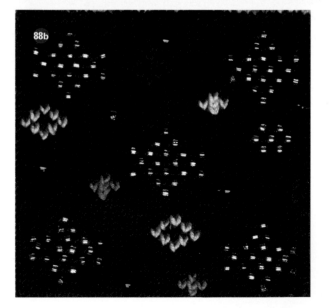

⑧⑨ Streamers

SIZE

6in × 6in (15cm × 15cm)

MATERIALS

1 pair US 5 (3.75mm/No. 9) needles
Cable needle

⑧⑨ₐ First colorway (× 8■)

Rowan Wool Cotton
1³⁄₄oz (50g) balls
purple (A)	⅕
yellow (B)	¹⁄₁₆
pink (C)	¹⁄₁₆
aqua (D)	¹⁄₁₆
red (E)	¹⁄₁₆

⑧⑨ᵦ Second colorway (× 4■)

Rowan Wool Cotton
1³⁄₄oz (50g) balls
aqua (A)	⅕
red (B)	¹⁄₁₆
purple (C)	¹⁄₁₆
pink (D)	¹⁄₁₆
yellow (E)	¹⁄₁₆

KNIT

Cast on 37 sts in the foll color sequence: 4A, 3B, 2C, 3A, 3D, 2E, 3A, 3B, 2C, 3A, 3D, 2E, 4A.
ROW 1 (RS): P4A, (inc once into each next 2 sts using E, K1D, inc once into next st using D, K1D, P3A, inc once into each next 2 sts using C, K1B, inc once into next st using B, K1B, P3A) twice, P1A (49 sts).

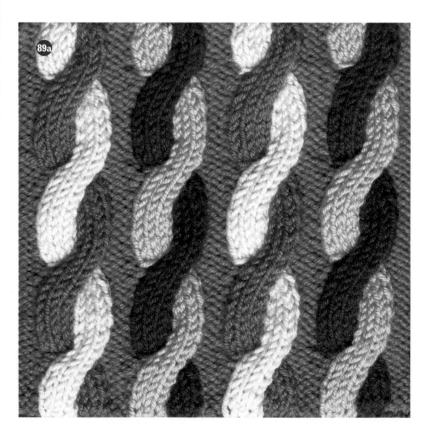

ROW 2 (WS): K4A, (P4B, P4C, K3A, P4D, P4E, K3A) twice, K1A.
ROW 3 (RS): P4A, (K4E, K4D, P3A, K4C, K4B, P3A) twice, P1A.
ROW 4 (WS): As row 2.
ROWS 5–8: Rep rows 3–4 twice.
ROW 9 (RS): P4A, (sl next 4 sts onto cable needle and hold at back of work, K4D, K the 4 sts on the cable needle using E, P3A, sl next 4 sts onto cable needle and hold at back of work, K4B, K the 4 sts on the cable needle using C, P3A) twice, P1A.
ROW 10 (WS): K4A, (P4C, P4B, K3A, P4E, P4D, K3A) twice, K1A.
Keeping color changes on cables correct, rep rows 3–4, 5 times, then rep rows 9–20 twice, then rep rows 9–14 once.
Keeping color changes on cables correct, rep rows 9–20 twice more, then rep rows 9–14 once more.
NEXT ROW (WS) (DEC): P4A, [K1E, (K2togE) twice, K2togD, K1D, P3A, K1C, (K2togC) twice, K2togB, K1B, P3A] twice, P1A
(37 sts).
(51 rows)
Bind (cast) off sts.

⑩ Sad clown

SIZE

6in × 6in (15cm × 15cm)

MATERIALS

1 pair US 5 (3.75mm/No. 9)
  needles

Single colorway (× 3⊞ ▣)

Rowan Wool Cotton
1¾oz (50g) balls

▨ green (A)		¼
☐ cream (B)		¹⁄₁₆
■ black (C)		¹⁄₅₀
■ pink (D)		¹⁄₅₀
■ red (E)		¹⁄₅₀
☐ yellow (F)		¹⁄₂₅
▨ purple (G)		¹⁄₅₀

Rowan Kidsilk Haze
(Used triple throughout)
1oz (25g) balls

■ bright pink (H)		¹⁄₂₅

(Used triple throughout)

⅛in (3mm) beads
◊ loop stitch with blue beads 33

☐ K on RS, P on WS
◉ make bobble (see page 123)

KNIT

Thread 34 blue beads onto H.
Note: When indicated on the chart, make a loop with a bead using H as folls: K next st leaving st on left needle, bring yarn forward between the needles, slide a bead up so that it is sitting about ¾in (2cm) away from the needle, and wrap the yarn with bead round thumb of left hand to make a loop, then take yarn between the needles to back of work and K the same stitch again, slipping st off left needle. Bring yarn forward between needles and then back over needle to WS of work. Lift the 2 sts just made off over this loop (see also page 122).
Cast on 37 sts and work until chart row 50 completed.
Bind (cast) off sts.

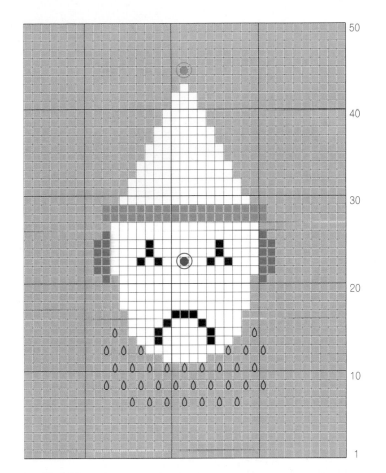

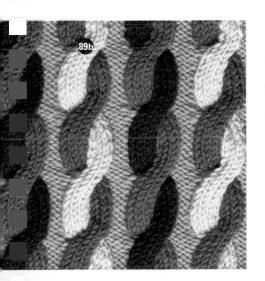

the four seasons

Images typically symbolic of the four seasons have been incorporated into this design, interspersed with cable stitch squares to form a distinctive layout. There is a hint of whimsy and humor in the choice of images, which lighten the mood. The four seasons is an enduring theme in art and music, and I have relished the challenge of bringing my own interpretation to this classic concept.

SIZE

52in × 52in (130cm × 130cm)

MATERIALS

1 pair US 5 (3.75mm/No. 9) needles
2 circular US 2–3 (3.00mm/No. 11) needles 32in (80cm) length
Cable needle

Yarn

Rowan Handknit DK Cotton
1¾oz (50g) balls

spearmint	5
orange	2
yellow	6
deep orange	1
white	2
bright blue	6
green	7
deep red	1
mid brown	1
red	2
deep green	2
lilac	1
purple	5
pink	5
black	1
mid blue	5

Quantities given for individual squares are approximate fractions of a ball.

Beads

⅛in (3mm) beads

silver	414

3/16in (5mm) beads

silver	60
black	12
red	44

GAUGE (TENSION)

22 sts and 30 rows to 4in (10cm) measured over stockinette (stocking) stitch using US 5 (3.75mm/No. 9) needles.

NOTE

Single stitch outlines on squares (91), (92), (93), (94), (96) and (98) can be Swiss-darned after knitting (see page 122).

ABBREVIATIONS

See page 127.

FINISHING

The sizes given for the finished afghan and individual squares are approximate. The number of stitches in a row, and the number of rows in a square differ in some instances. Therefore, when sewing pieces together, ease the extra stitches or rows into the adjoining square.

Press the individual squares using a damp cloth and a warm iron. Sew the squares together, joining bound- (cast-) off edge of one square to the cast-on edge of the next square, easing in stitches, if necessary, to form vertical strips. Sew the vertical strips together, easing in rows, if necessary, to create one block.

Edging

MATERIALS

2 circular US 2–3 (3.00mm/No. 11) needles 32in (80cm) length

Yarn

Rowan Handknit DK Cotton
1¾oz (50g) balls

deep orange	3

KNIT

With RS facing, pick up and knit 288 sts along the RH edge of the afghan.
Beg with a WS row, cont to work in garter stitch (knit every row) for 6 rows, inc 1 st at each end of all WS rows.
Bind (cast) off sts knitwise.
Rep for LH edge of the afghan.
With RS facing, pick up and knit 285 sts along bottom edge of the afghan.
Rep edging as for RH and LH edges.
Rep for top edge of afghan.
Neatly sew border edges together.

Order of squares

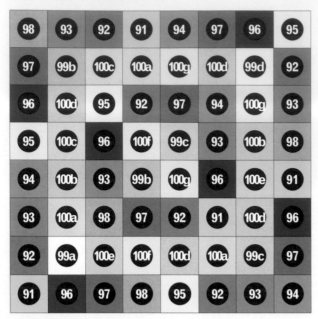

QUANTITY OF SQUARES

⑨¹ Chick		4
⑨² Summer sunshine		6
⑨³ Leaf		6
⑨⁴ Christmas tree		4
⑨⁵ Tulip		4
⑨⁶ Strawberry		6
⑨⁷ Halloween		6
⑨⁸ Snowman		4
⑨⁹ Four seasons cable		1
	⑨⁹ᵃ First colorway	1
	⑨⁹ᵇ Second colorway	2
	⑨⁹ᶜ Third colorway	2
	⑨⁹ᵈ Fourth colorway	1
¹⁰⁰ Four seasons cable		2
	¹⁰⁰ᵃ First colorway	3
	¹⁰⁰ᵇ Second colorway	2
	¹⁰⁰ᶜ Third colorway	2
	¹⁰⁰ᵈ Fourth colorway	4
	¹⁰⁰ᵉ Fifth colorway	2
	¹⁰⁰ᶠ Sixth colorway	2
	¹⁰⁰ᵍ Seventh colorway	3

⑨¹ Chick

SIZE
6½in × 6½in (16.5cm x 16.5cm)

MATERIALS
1 pair US 5 (3.75mm/No. 9)
   needles

Single colorway (× 4⊞ ▣)
Rowan Handknit DK Cotton
1¾oz (50g) balls
☐ spearmint (A)   ⅓
☐ orange (B)   ¹/₁₀
☐ yellow (C)   ¹/₁₆
☐ deep orange (D)   ¹/₅₀

³/₁₆in (5mm) beads
● black   1

☐ K on RS, P on WS

KNIT
Thread 1 black bead onto yarn C.
Cast on 38 sts and work until
chart row 50 completed.
Bind (cast) off sts.

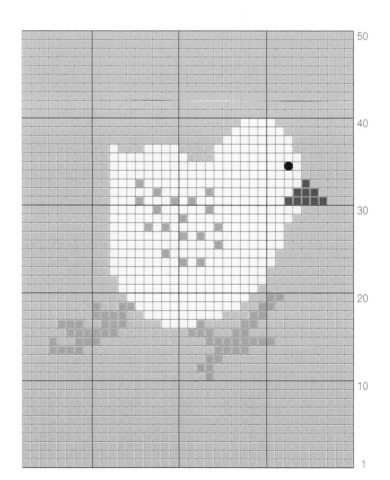

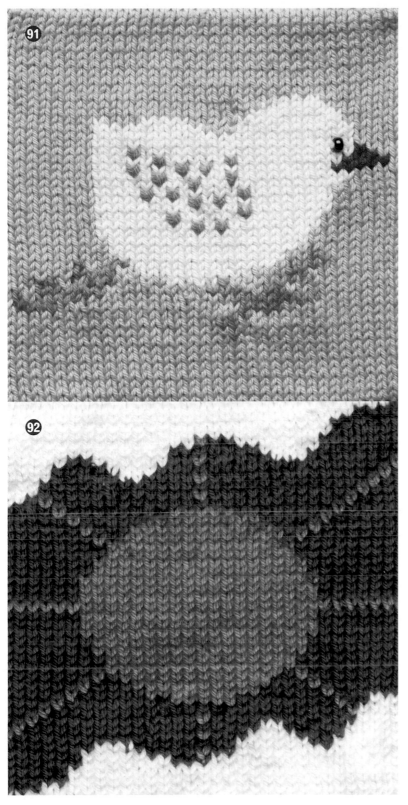

⑫ Summer sunshine

SIZE
6½in × 6½in (16.5cm × 16.5cm)

MATERIALS
1 pair US 5 (3.75mm/No. 9)
   needles

Single colorway (× 6⊞ ▣)
Rowan Handknit DK Cotton
1¾oz (50g) balls
☐ white   ⅙
■ bright blue   ⅕
■ orange   ⅛

☐ K on RS, P on WS

KNIT
Cast on 37 sts and work until
chart row 50 completed.
Bind (cast) off sts.

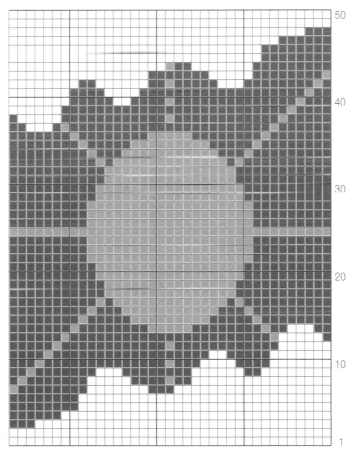

⑨③ Leaf

SIZE
6½in × 6½in (16.5cm × 16.5cm)

MATERIALS
1 pair US 5 (3.75mm/No. 9)
   needles

Single colorway (× 6⊞ ▣)
Rowan Handknit DK Cotton
1¾oz (50g) balls

- ▨ green   ⅓
- ▨ deep orange   ¹⁄₅₀
- ▨ deep red   ⅛
- ▨ mid brown   ¹⁄₅₀

☐ K on RS, P on WS

KNIT
Cast on 38 sts and work until
chart row 50 completed.
Bind (cast) off sts.

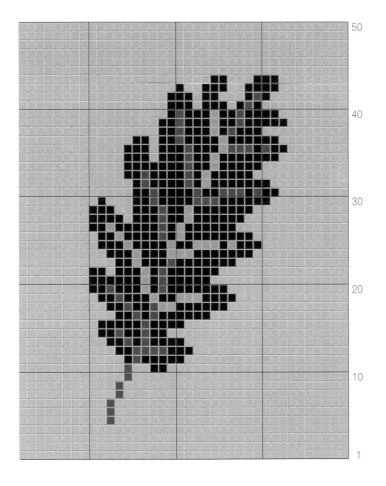

⑨④ Christmas tree

SIZE
6½in × 6½in (16.5cm × 16.5cm)

MATERIALS
1 pair US 5 (3.75mm/No. 9)
   needles

Single colorway (× 4⊞ ▣)
Rowan Handknit DK Cotton
1¾oz (50g) balls

- ▨ bright blue (A)   ⅓
- ▨ red (B)   ¹⁄₅₀
- ▨ deep green (C)   ¹⁄₁₆
- ▨ green (D)   ¹⁄₅₀
- ☐ yellow (E)   ¹⁄₅₀

³⁄₁₆in (5mm) beads
- ● red   10

◉ silver

☐ K on RS, P on WS

KNIT
Thread 10 red beads onto C and 6
silver beads onto A.
Cast on 37 sts and work until
chart row 50 completed.
Bind (cast) off sts.

Using the photograph as a guide,
embroider star at top of Christmas
tree using E.

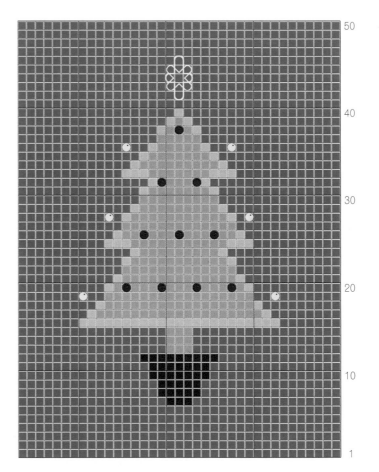

🅖🅕 Tulip

SIZE
6½in × 6½in (16.5cm × 16.5cm)

MATERIALS
1 pair US 5 (3.75mm/No. 9)
  needles

Single colorway (× 4⊞ ▣)
Rowan Handknit DK Cotton
1¾oz (50g) balls

☐ yellow	⅓
▨ deep green	1/16
▨ green	1/16
▨ purple	1/25
▨ lilac	1/25

☐ K on RS, P on WS

KNIT
Cast on 37 sts and work until
chart row 50 completed.
Bind (cast) off sts.

🅖🅖 Strawberry

SIZE
6½in × 6½in (16.5cm × 16.5cm)

MATERIALS
1 pair US 5 (3.75mm/No. 9)
  needles

Single colorway (× 6⊞ ▣)
Rowan Handknit DK Cotton
1¾oz (50g) balls

▨ pink (A)	⅓
■ red (B)	⅛
☐ yellow (C)	1/50
▨ green (D)	1/16
▨ dark green (E)	1/50

3/16in (5mm) beads
⬤ silver   6
⅛in (3mm) beads
◉ silver   11
☐ K on RS, P on WS

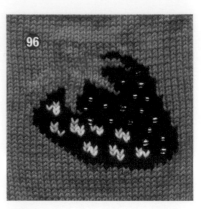

KNIT
Thread beads onto B in the foll
sequence: 2 small, 1 large, 5
small, 2 large, 1 small, 1 large, 3
small, 2 large.
Cast on 37 sts and work until
chart row 50 completed.
Bind (cast) off sts.

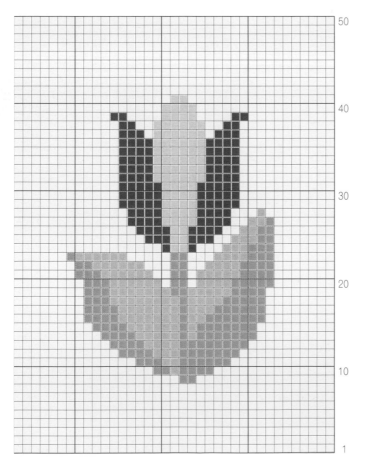

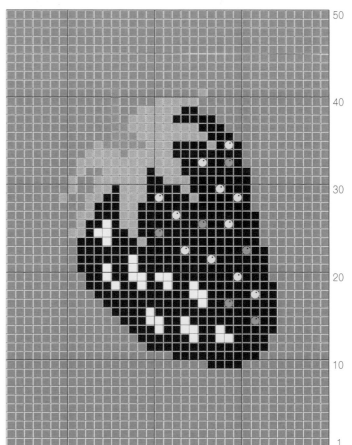

97 Halloween

SIZE
6½in × 6½in (16.5cm × 16.5cm)

MATERIALS
1 pair US 5 (3.75mm/No. 9)
   needles

Single colorway (× 6⊞ ▣)
Rowan Handknit DK Cotton
1¾oz (50g) balls

- ■ purple   ²/₅
- ▨ orange   ⅛
- ■ black   ¹/₂₅
- ▨ dark green   ¹/₅₀
- ▨ green   ¹/₅₀
- □ K on RS, P on WS

KNIT
Cast on 38 sts and work until
chart row 50 completed.
Bind (cast) off sts.

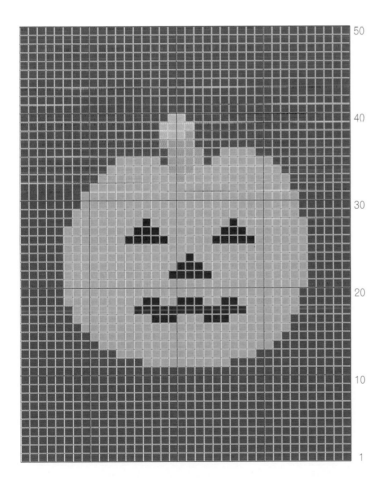

98 Snowman

SIZE
6½in × 6½in (16.5cm × 16.5cm)

MATERIALS
1 pair US 5 (3.75mm/No. 9)
  needles

Single colorway (× 4⊞ ▣)
Rowan Handknit DK Cotton
1¾oz (50g) balls

☐	white (A)	⅙
▨	mid blue (B)	¼
■	red (C)	¹⁄₂₅
■	black (D)	¹⁄₂₅
☐	yellow (E)	¹⁄₅₀
■	deep orange (F)	¹⁄₅₀

⅛in (3mm) beads
◉ silver   87
³⁄₁₆in (5mm) beads
● black   2
● red   1

☐ K on RS, P on WS

KNIT
Thread beads onto A in the
following sequence: 87 silver,
2 black.
Cast on 37 sts and work until
chart row 50 completed.
Bind (cast) off sts.

Using the photograph as a guide
embroider nose onto snowman
using F.

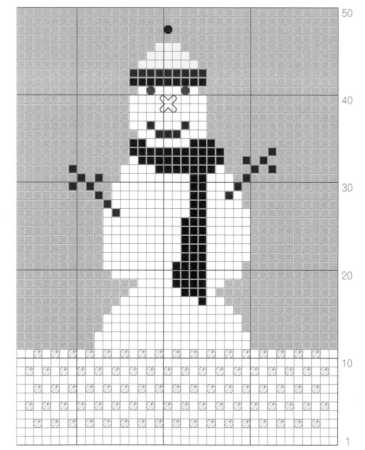

99 Four seasons cable 1

SIZE
6½in × 6½in (16.5cm × 16.5cm)

MATERIALS
1 pair US 5 (3.75mm/No. 9)
  needles
Cable needle

99a First colorway (× 1 ▣)
Rowan Handknit DK Cotton
1¾oz (50g) balls
  yellow   ³⁄₅

99b Second colorway (× 2 ▣)
Rowan Handknit DK Cotton
1¾oz (50g) balls
  bright blue   ³⁄₅

99c Third colorway (× 2 ▣)
Rowan Handknit DK Cotton
1¾oz (50g) balls
  mid blue   ³⁄₅

99d Fourth colorway (× 1 ▣)
Rowan Handknit DK Cotton
1¾oz (50g) balls
  spearmint   ³⁄₅

99a

KNIT

Cast on 38 sts.

ROW 1 (RS) (INC): **P3, (K1, inc once into each next 2 sts, K1, P3) 5 times (48 sts).**

ROW 2 (WS): **K3, (P2, K2, P2, K3) 5 times.**

ROW 3 (RS): **P3, (K2, P2, K2, P3) 5 times.**

ROW 4 (WS): **As row 2.**

ROWS 5–6: **Rep rows 3–4.**

ROW 7 (RS): **P3, (sl next 4 sts onto cable needle and hold at front of work, K2, then put 2 sts back onto LH needle and purl them, then K2 from cable needle, P3) 5 times.**

ROW 8 (WS): **As row 2.**

ROWS 9–16: **Rep rows 3–4, 4 times.**

Rep rows 7–16, 3 times more.

Rep rows 7–10 once more.

NEXT ROW (RS) (DEC): **P3, (K1, K2tog twice, K1, P3) 5 times (38 sts).**

(51 rows)

Bind (cast) off sts.

99b

99c

99d

⓵⓪⓪ Four seasons cable 2

SIZE

6½in × 6½in (16.5cm × 16.5cm)

GAUGE (TENSION)

1 pair US 5 (3.75mm/No. 9) needles
Cable needle

⓵⓪⓪ First colorway (× 3◼)
Rowan Handknit DK Cotton
1¾oz (50g) balls
pink   ³/₅

⓵⓪⓪ᵇ Second colorway (× 2◼)
Rowan Handknit DK Cotton
1¾oz (50g) balls
purple   ³/₅

⓵⓪⓪ᶜ Third colorway (× 2◼)
Rowan Handknit DK Cotton
1¾oz (50g) balls
mid blue   ³/₅

⓵⓪⓪ᵈ Fourth colorway (× 4◼)
Rowan Handknit DK Cotton
1¾oz (50g) balls
green   ³/₅

⓵⓪⓪ᵉ Fifth colorway (× 2◼)
Rowan Handknit DK Cotton
1¾oz (50g) balls
bright blue   ³/₅

⓵⓪⓪ᶠ Sixth colorway (× 2◼)
Rowan Handknit DK Cotton
1¾oz (50g) balls
spearmint   ³/₅

⓵⓪⓪ᵍ Seventh colorway (× 3◼)
Rowan Handknit DK Cotton
1¾oz (50g) balls
yellow   ³/₅

KNIT

Cast on 38 sts.

ROW 1 (RS) (INC): **P3, (K1, inc once into each next 2 sts, K1, P3) 5 times (48 sts).**

ROW 2 (WS): **K3, (P2, K2, P2, K3) 5 times.**

ROW 3 (RS): **P3, (K2, P2, K2, P3) 5 times.**

ROW 4 (WS): **As row 2.**

ROWS 5–6: **Rep rows 3–4.**

ROW 7 (RS): **P3, (sl next 4 sts onto cable needle and hold at back of work, K2, then put 2 sts back onto LH needle and purl them, then K2 from cable needle, P3) 5 times.**

ROW 8 (WS): **As row 2.**

ROWS 9–16: **Rep rows 3–4, 4 times.**

Rep rows 7–16, 3 times more.

Rep rows 7–10 once more.

NEXT ROW (RS) (DEC): **P3, (K1, K2tog twice, K1, P3) 5 times (38 sts).**

(51 rows)

Bind (cast) off sts.

100a

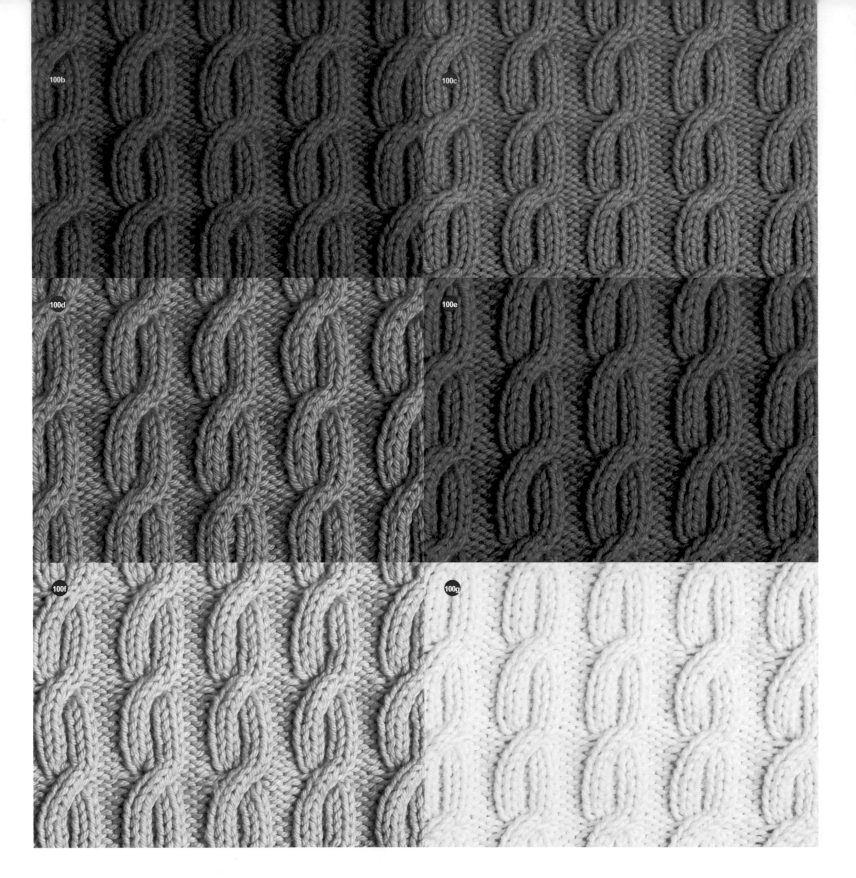

100b   100c
100d   100e
100f   100g

Techniques

INTARSIA KNITTING

Intarsia knitting produces a single thickness fabric that uses different balls of yarn for different areas of color. There should be very little, if any, carrying across of yarns at the back of the work.

Joining in a new color

1 Work up to the stitch before the new color is required. Lay the new yarn that is to be joined in over the right hand needle, keeping it close to the needle.

2 Work the next stitch using the yarn that is already joined in: as the yarn is pulled up and around the needle to make the stitch, the new yarn is trapped into the work, ready to use for the next stitch.

Changing colors

To avoid gaps between stitches when changing color, it is essential that the two yarns are crossed over at the back of the work.

1 On a knit row, insert the right needle into the next stitch. Place the old purple yarn over the new pink yarn. Pull the new pink yarn up and knit the stitch.

2 On a purl row, insert the right needle into the next stitch. Place the old pink yarn over the new purple yarn. Pull the new purple yarn up and purl the next stitch.

Darning in ends

When an intarsia square is completed there will be loose ends to darn in on the back of the work.

1 Darn the ends around shapes by darning through the loops of the same color in one direction first.

2 Then darn the end back on itself, stretching the work before cutting the end of the yarn.

FAIR ISLE KNITTING

Fair Isle knitting produces a double thickness of fabric. In traditional Fair Isle designs, two different colored yarns are used in each row creating a small busy repeat pattern. As the row is worked, the yarn that is not being used is stranded across the back of the work. It is important to keep the work elastic by making sure that the yarns are not pulled too tight. This can be achieved by keeping the stitches at the correct width on the needle at all times whilst knitting. To avoid long loops at the back of the work, yarns should not be stranded over more than three stitches at a time.

Stranding technique

This method is used in a pattern repeat where the changeover between the two colors is three stitches or less at a time. The unused yarn is carried across the back of the work.

1 On a knit row, insert the needle into the next stitch and pick up yarn 1, taking it under yarn 2 to knit the next stitch.

2 When you are ready to change color, insert the needle into the next stitch and pick up yarn 2, taking it over yarn 1 to knit the next stitch.

3 On a purl row, insert the needle into the next stitch and pick up yarn 1, taking it under yarn 2 to purl the next stitch.

4 When you are ready to change color, insert the needle into the next stitch and pick up yarn 2, taking it over yarn 1 to purl the next stitch.

5 Keep this over and under sequence of picking up the yarns consistent on every row to avoid the yarns tangling together. It will also help to create a neat, flat fabric.

Weaving technique

This method is used in a pattern repeat where the changeover between the two colors is four stitches or more at a time. The unused yarn is woven into the back of the work.

1 On a knit row, insert the right needle into the next stitch and pick up the yarn from under that is to be woven into the work. Place it across the tips of the needles and hold onto it firmly at the back of the work.

2 Take yarn 1 around the right needle to knit the next stitch. As the new loop is brought through the old loop, lift yarn 2 up and out of the way so that it is not caught by the right needle.

3 Hold down yarn 2 at the back of the work whilst working the next stitch. The yarn has been woven in across the back of two stitches.

4 On a purl row, insert the needle into the next stitch and pick up the yarn from under that is to be woven into the work. Place it across the tips of the needles and hold onto it firmly.

5 Take yarn 1 around the right needle to purl the next stitch. As the new loop is brought through the old loop, lift yarn 2 up and out of the way so that it is not caught by the right needle.

6 Hold down yarn 2 at the back of the work whilst working the next stitch. The yarn has been woven in across the back of two stitches.

KNITTING WITH BEADS

There are many different types of bead available, but not all of them are suitable for hand-knitting. When choosing beads it is important to check that the bead hole is big enough for the yarn to pass through. In addition the weight and size of the beads also needs to be considered. For example, large heavy beads on 4-ply knitting will look clumsy and cause the fabric to sag. It is also wise to check whether the beads you are using are washable, as some may not be.

When you have chosen your beads, you must thread them onto the yarn before you start to knit. There is a very easy way to do this.

Threading beads onto yarn

Place a length of sewing cotton beneath the yarn, then bring the two ends of the cotton together and thread both ends through a sewing needle. Thread the beads onto the needle, then push them down the sewing cotton and onto the knitting yarn. Remember that the first bead you thread onto the yarn will be the last one to be knitted in.

ADDING BEADS WITH A SLIP STITCH

This is my preferred method of adding beads to knitting, and it works on both wrong-side and right-side rows. The beads sit in front of a slipped stitch and hang down slightly from where they are knitted in. I have found that if the yarn is held quite firmly and the next stitch after the bead is knitted tightly, the bead sits very neatly and snugly against the knitting.

Adding beads on a right side row

1 Work to where the bead is to be placed. Bring the yarn forward between the points of the needles.

2 Push a bead up the yarn to the front of the work, so that it rests in front of the right-hand needle.

3 Slip the next stitch purlwise from the left-hand to the right-hand needle, leaving the bead in front of the slipped stitch.

4 Take the yarn between the needles to the back of the work and continue in pattern. The bead is now secured in position.

Adding beads on a wrong side row
When beads are placed on a wrong side row the instructions are almost the same.

1 When a bead is to be added, take the yarn back between the needle points and push a bead up to the front of the work.

2 Slip the next stitch exactly as above.

3 Bring the yarn forward and continue working. On the next row work the slip stitch firmly.

KNITTING WITH SEQUINS

Although using sequins in hand knitting has been practiced for many years, I only started to experiment with them on recent projects. Sequins not only add extra color and sparkle to a knitted fabric, but they also change the quality and feel of the knitting. The all-over sequinned square in the Fish afghan feels like soft fish scales and creates a very tactile piece of fabric.

When choosing sequins it is important to remember that the hole through the center must be big enough for the yarn to pass through. The size of the sequin should also be considered, and chosen in relation to the weight of yarn used. And, as with beads, it is also best to check if the sequins are washable before buying them.

The method of adding sequins to knitting is identical to the way that beads are knitted in. However, care should be taken to hold the sequins flat to the fabric while knitting, ensuring that they are all laying the same way. And it is advisable only to place sequins while working on a right side row, as it is extremely difficult to do this on a wrong side row.

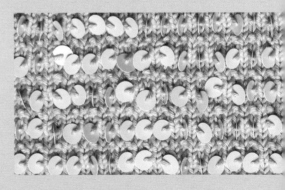

ADDING EMBROIDERY TO KNITTING

Outlines, single dots or fancy shapes and textures can be added to your fabric after knitting. It is advisable to finish your knitting and tidy up the loose ends before embroidering. A large, blunt darning needle should be used to avoid splitting the stitches. A yarn of the same or a slightly heavier weight as the main knitting that will easily cover the stitches is recommended.

I have used Swiss darning in various projects in this book. This is a method of duplicating knitted stitches on stockinette (stocking) stitch fabrics using a needle and a separate length of yarn. It is a quick and easy way of adding dashes of color or outlines, and it can be worked horizontally or vertically.

Swiss-darning (worked horizontally)

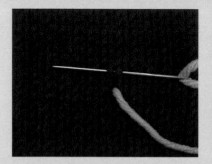

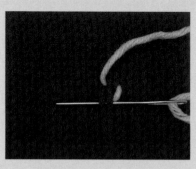

1 From the back of the work, insert the needle through the base of the knitted stitch, then take the needle around the top of the knitted stitch.

2 From the front of the work, insert the needle into the base of the same knitted stitch and out through the base of the next knitted stitch on the left.

Swiss-darning (worked vertically)

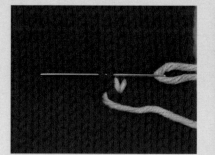

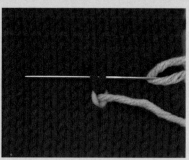

3 Pull the yarn through. You have now covered a stitch. Repeat the process until you have completed the work.

1 Darn the first stitch as for horizontal darning, but bring the needle out through the base of the stitch above the one just worked. Work that stitch in the same way.

Continue forming the stitches, but work upwards rather than from right to left.

LOOP STITCH

Loops of yarn can be knitted into a garter stitch background to create a pile fabric. A loop is made on the RS of the work as follows.

1 Knit next stitch but leave it on the left-hand needle. Bring yarn forward between needles.

2 Wrap the yarn around your thumb to make a loop.

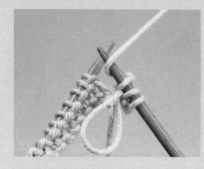

3 Then take yarn back between the needles and knit the same stitch again, this time slipping the stitch off the left-hand needle and the loop off your thumb. This will create an extra stitch.

4 Bring yarn forward between the needles and then back over the needle to the WS of the work. This will create another extra stitch.

5 Lift the first stitch in the sequence over the last two. Then lift the second stitch in the sequence over the last one. Continue knitting until the next loop is required.

CABLES

Cables are the crossing of one set of stitches over another to create a twisted rope effect. Stitches can be crossed over at the front or the back of the work; this determines whether the cable twists to the left or to the right. Stitches held at the front of the work will twist the cable to the left, stitches held at the back of the work will twist the cable to the right. Cables are usually knitted in stockinette (stocking) stitch on a background of reverse stockinette (stocking) stitch, though a background of stockinette (stocking) stitch can also work well. Usually the number of stitches that are crossed are half of the amount stated in the abbreviation, ie: c8b means cross 4 stitches with 4 stitches. There are many different variations, so it is best to read the instructions carefully before starting to knit. This example shows how to work c8b.

c8b

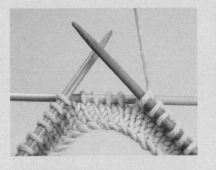

1 Slip the next 4 stitches onto the cable needle and hold at the back of the work.

2 Knit 4 stitches from the left-hand needle.

3 Then knit the 4 stitches that are on the cable needle.

Make sure that you pull the yarn firmly and knit the stitches tightly to avoid any gaps in the work.

BOBBLES

There are many different ways to create bobbles in knitting, but this is my preferred method. It involves making several stitches out of one stitch by knitting into the front and the back of the stitch several times on a RS row, and then knitting and purling these stitches to create an extra bit of fabric that becomes the bobble.

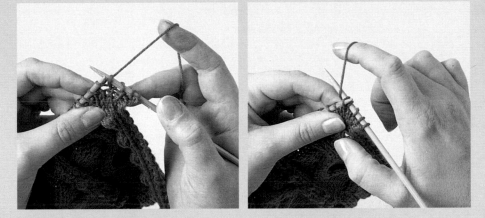

1 Knit into the front, back, front, back, front of the next stitch, before releasing the stitch off the left needle.

2 Turn the work around so that the WS is facing. Purl the five stitches, pulling firmly on the yarn after the first stitch.

3 Turn the work again so that the RS is facing. Knit the five stitches, again pulling firmly on the yarn after the first stitch.

4 Lift the 2nd, 3rd, 4th and 5th stitches off over the 1st stitch.

5 Push the bobble to the front of the work, and pull firmly on the yarn to tighten it up.

PIECING TOGETHER YOUR AFGHAN

After spending many hours knitting the squares for your afghan it is very important that the sewing together of the squares is done as neatly as possible. I would recommend that mattress stitch is used, because it is easy to learn, very precise and it creates almost invisible seams. One big advantage of using this stitch over other methods of sewing up is that you work with the right sides of the knitting facing up towards you, which enables you to see exactly how the seam is progressing.

A blunt sewing-up needle and a matching yarn should be used to sew together the squares. Lay the pieces of knitting out on a flat surface in the order in which they are to be pieced together. I would advise that the squares are sewn together to create vertical strips, then the vertical strips sewn together to create a block.

Mattress stitch seam (sewing stitches to stitches)

1 From the back of the work, insert the needle through the center of the first stitch along one of the edges, leaving a long tail of yarn.

2 From the back of the work, insert the needle between the first and the second stitches along the opposite edge.

3 Continue in this way, zigzagging backwards and forwards from edge to edge, and pulling the stitches up to close the seam. Do not pull too hard or the seam will be too tight.

The mattress seam is invisible on the right side. Continue sewing the whole seam, then secure the ends by darning them in.

Mattress stitch seam (sewing rows to rows)

1 From the front, insert the needle between the first and second stitches on the first row. Take the needle under the next row and bring it through to the front again. Pull the yarn through, leaving a long end. Insert the needle the same way into the other edge that is to be joined, but this time bring the needle out two rows above the point where it goes in.

2 Insert the needle into the first edge again, into the same hole that the thread last came out from on that edge. Bring the needle out two rows above that point.

3 Insert the needle into the second edge again, into the same hole that the thread last came out from on that edge. Bring the needle out two rows above that point.

4 Repeat, zigzagging from edge to edge for about 1in (2.5cm). Pull the thread up, holding the seam and long end of the yarn with the left hand.

PICKING UP STITCHES

Stitches will have to be picked up along all four edges of the knitted squares once they are pieced together, to create the edgings.
It is important that they are picked up neatly and evenly to ensure that the edgings lay flat. Before picking up the stitches, it is advisable to work out how many stitches will need to be picked up along each square to achieve the total for the entire length that is stated in the pattern.

Picking up stitches along a bound (cast) off edge
1   With right side facing, insert a needle through the middle of the stitch directly below the bound (cast) off edge.

2   Take the yarn around the needle and pull it through the middle of this stitch to create a new stitch.

Picking up stitches along a cast-on edge
1   With right side facing (so the work is held upside down), insert a needle through the middle of the stitch directly above the cast on edge.

2   Take the yarn around the needle and pull it through the middle of this stitch to create a new stitch.

Picking up stitches along a selvedge (side edge)
1   With right side facing, insert a needle through the fabric from front to back, one whole stitch in from the edge of the work.

2   Take the yarn around the needle and pull the loop through to create a new stitch.

BLOCKING AND PRESSING

The blocking and pressing of knitted panels is an essential part of the finishing process, and one that is often omitted by knitters. There are several reasons why blocking and pressing should be done. Firstly, it flattens the edges of the knitting, which makes it easier to pick up stitches or sew together panels. Secondly, it ensures that the panels are of the correct measurement. And lastly, it finishes the knitted fabric, and in most cases changes the physical quality of the knitting, smoothing out stitches and making the fabric feel softer and more fluid.

Blocking is the pinning out of the knitted pieces, which should be done on a flat surface with the wrong side facing up. A tape measure should be used to ensure that the pieces are of the correct size. The temperature of the iron used for pressing is dependant on the fiber content of the yarn, as is the damp or dry pressing cloth, which must completely cover the panel that is going to be pressed. The general rule is as follows: natural fibers require a damp pressing cloth and a warm iron, and synthetic fibers and mixes require a dry pressing cloth and a cool iron. However, not all yarns conform to these rules and some have alternative requirements, so it is always advisable to read the pressing instructions that are printed on the ball band. If several different yarns have been used in one piece of knitting, it is better to play safe and follow the instructions for the most delicate yarn. If the heat of the iron is too hot, it could ruin the knitting permanently, resulting in a limp and lifeless piece of knitting that is irreversible.

After pressing, it is best to leave the knitting pinned out for at least half an hour to allow all of the heat and moisture to evaporate. Then, when the pins are removed, the knitting will be flat and ready for sewing up.

Tip: If you are working on one of the set projects in this book and therefore you know the layout of the afghan, an alternative method of piecing together the squares can be used.

After you have completed a square and the stitches are bound (cast) off, begin the next square above it by picking up the required number of stitches along the bound (cast) off edge of the previous square.

If the first row of the next square is stockinette (stocking) stitch, you will have completed the first row of this square after picking up the stitches. Therefore, the next row, with wrong side facing you, will be row two of the next square.

If the first row of the next square is textured, or it involves increasing into the stitches, for example, for a cable pattern, pick up the stitches along the bound (cast) off edge of the previous square, and then slide the stitches back onto the left needle so that the right side is facing you again. You will then be beginning with row one of the next square, after picking up the stitches.

Repeat this with each square until a strip is completed. The sewing together of the individual squares stitch by stitch is avoided, and you will only have the vertical seams to sew together to complete the afghan.

WASHING AND CARING FOR YOUR AFGHAN

Hand-washing
Your hand-knitted afghan will need to be treated with extra care and ideally should be hand-washed to maintain its quality. Because of the size of an afghan, it is perhaps better to use the bath or a similar large vessel to wash it in. Use plenty of lukewarm water and a soft detergent that is specially formulated for knitwear. The fabric should be gently squeezed and then rinsed in several changes of water to get rid of all of the soap. Special care should be taken when lifting the afghan out of the water as it could easily stretch and distort if it is not supported properly. It is a good idea to get rid of some of the excess water by gently spinning the afghan in a washing machine. However, it must first be placed inside a large secure wash-bag, such as a duvet-cover, to avoid the fabric stretching while in the machine. This will also protect beads, buttons and sequins if they have been used. A large washing machine will be required if the afghan is one of the larger designs.

Lay the afghan out flat on towels or blankets after washing, and gently ease back into shape. It should then be left alone until it is completely dry.

Dry-cleaning
Perhaps an easier way to clean your afghan is to have it professionally dry-cleaned. But before taking it to the cleaners, check on all of the ball bands of the yarns that have been used that they can be dry-cleaned. And also remember that if beads, sequins or buttons have been used, the dry-cleaners may refuse to clean it for you.

yarn information

If you want your knitted afghan to look like the picture in the book, I would recommend that you use the yarns that I have specified for each design. A substitute yarn that differs in weight, shade or fiber content will change the whole look, feel and size of the finished piece of knitting.

Alternatively this book gives you the option to create your own unique designs by mixing and matching squares from any of the twelve afghans. But if you wish to take on this challenge, there are a few guidelines that must be followed to ensure successful results.

CHOOSING THE RIGHT WEIGHT OF YARN

Each individual project uses either one type of yarn, or combines a few together that are of identical weights. This ensures that all of the squares within a project knit up to the same size. This becomes crucial when the individual squares are pieced together. If you wish to mix and match squares from different afghans to create your own design, it is essential that you choose one weight of yarn to knit up all of the squares. For example, you may wish to combine "Mother of Pearl" from Afternoon Tea, which uses a lightweight double-knit cotton, with "Peel" from Fruity, which uses a chunky cotton. These two squares will not knit up to the same size because the chunky weight yarn is thicker than the lightweight double-knit yarn. Therefore, one yarn must be selected for the whole project and used to knit up all of the squares in that project. If the chunky weight yarn is used, it will create a much bigger afghan than if the lightweight double-knit yarn is used.

QUANTITIES OF YARN AND DYE LOTS

At the beginning of each project the quantities of yarn are given for the whole afghan. The amounts of yarn are then further broken down for each individual square. If mixing and matching squares from different projects, these quantities will alter. This is because the length of a ball of yarn depends on its weight and fiber content: an aran weight cotton will have a shorter length than an aran weight wool, and a 4-ply cotton will have a longer length than a double-knit cotton. The quantities of yarn can be re-calculated if desired, but many of the squares in this book use very small amounts of yarn – oddments in a lot of cases – and so my advice would be to purchase one ball of each of the colors that are needed, and then to purchase more as and when required. The worry of odd dye lots is far less important if a multi-colored design is being knitted, and so the yarn does not have to be bought in one go. In fact, slight variations in dye lots can add an unexpected twist to the overall look of the afghan, and contribute to the "patchwork" effect. Even Denim Hearts, which is knitted using a denim-look yarn in three shades, could look very interesting if different dye lots are used. An exception to this is Floor Coverings, which is knitted in one color. In this case, dye lots will matter, and it is advisable to purchase sufficient yarn in the same dye lot to complete the project.

DIFFERENCES IN STITCHES AND ROWS

There are slight differences in the number of stitches and rows in some of the individual squares. This is due to a number of reasons, some of which are design-based and some which are technical. For example, in order to center a motif, sometimes an odd number of stitches and rows is required and sometimes an even number is required, depending on the shape. The centering of motifs is a fundamental part of my designing – a discipline that is also applied to the pattern repeats in my work. In other cases it is the stitches themselves that dictate the number of stitches and rows that are required to create a knitted square of a particular size. Cable designs require more stitches than plain stockinette (stocking) stitch fabrics due to the crossing over of the stitches, which inevitably pulls the knitting in. And seed (moss) stitch fabrics tend to condense down the rows, so that often more rows are needed than if plain stockinette (stocking) stitch is being knitted. When piecing together the individual squares, the difference of a few stitches or rows will not effect the finished result. In almost all garment knitting the easing together of pieces of knitting is quite common practice; for example, a fitted sleeve will often have to be eased into the armhole. I would recommend that a method of sewing up called mattress stitch is used to piece together the squares. This is a method that enables you to ease knitted fabrics together. Instructions for this technique can be found on page 124.

GAUGE (TENSION) AND SELECTING CORRECT NEEDLE SIZE

The needle sizes that I have recommended for each design have been chosen to create a firm gauge (tension). This is especially important if you are knitting accessories that are going to be handled, such as cushions, bags and afghans. If the knitting is too loose, the article will easily become misshapen, and will most likely drop and grow in size. Using a slightly smaller needle than the usual recommended size for the yarn ensures that the knitted fabric retains its shape.

Gauge (tension) can differ quite dramatically between knitters. This is because of the way that the needles and the yarn are held. So if your gauge (tension) does not match that stated in the pattern, you should change your needle size following this simple rule. If your knitting is too loose, your gauge (tension) will read that you have fewer stitches and rows than the given gauge (tension), and you will need to change to a thinner needle to make the stitch size smaller. Alternatively, if your knitting is too tight, your gauge (tension) will read that you have more stitches and rows than the given gauge (tension), and you will need to change to a thicker needle to make the stitch size bigger.

It should be noted that if the projects in this book are not knitted to the correct gauge (tension), yarn quantities will be effected.

YARNS USED IN THIS BOOK

A selection of yarns from the Rowan Yarn collection have been used to knit all of the afghans in this book. Below is a guide to the yarns that I have used, specifying their weight, length and fiber content.

Glace Cotton
Lightweight cotton yarn
100% cotton
Approximately 125yd (115m) per 1
¾oz (50g) ball

All Seasons Cotton
Aran-weight cotton and microfiber yarn
60% cotton/ 40% microfiber
Approximately 98yd (90m) per 1
¾oz (50g) ball

Rowan Denim
Medium-weight cotton yarn
100% cotton
Approximately 101yd (93m) per 1
¾oz (50g) ball

Handknit DK Cotton
Medium-weight cotton yarn
100% cotton
Approximately 101yd (93m) per 1
¾oz (50g) ball

Wool Cotton
Double-knitting-weight wool and cotton yarn
50% merino wool/ 50% cotton
Approximately 123yd (113m) per 1
¾oz (50g) ball

Lurex Shimmer
Very lightweight lurex yarn
80% viscose/ 20% polyester
Approximately 104yd (95m) per 1oz (25g) ball

Kidsilk Haze
Very lightweight mohair yarn
70% super kid mohair/ 30% silk
Approximately 230yd (210m) per 1oz (25g) ball

Plaid
Chunky-weight wool yarn
42% merino wool/ 30% acrylic fiber/ 28% superfine alpaca

Approximately 109 yd (100m) per 3 ¼oz (100g) ball

Yorkshire Tweed DK
Medium-weight wool yarn
100% pure new wool
Approximately 123yd (113m) per 1
¾oz (50g) ball

Cotton Rope
Chunky-weight cotton yarn
55% cotton/ 45% acrylic
Approximately 63yd (58m) per 1
¾oz (50g) ball

CONVERSIONS
Needle sizes

US SIZE	METRIC SIZE	OLD UK & CANADIAN SIZE
15	10	000
13	9	00
11	8	0
11	7½	1
10½	7	2
10½	6½	3
10	6	4
9	5½	5
8	5	6
7	4½	7
6	4	8
5	3¾	9
4	3½	–
3	3¼	10
2–3	3	11
2	2¾	12
1	2¼	13
0	2	14

Weights and lengths

oz	=	g × 0.0352
g	=	oz × 28.35
in	=	cm × 0.3937
cm	=	in × 2.54
yd	=	m × 0.9144
m	=	yd × 1.0936

ABBREVIATIONS

beg	beginning/begin
cont	continue
cm	centimeter
c4f	cable 4 front: slip next 2 sts onto cable needle and hold at front of work, K2, then K2 sts from the cable needle
c4b	cable 4 back: slip next 2 sts onto cable needle and hold at back of work, K2, then K2 sts from the cable needle
c6f	cable 6 front: slip next 3 sts onto cable needle and hold at front of work, K3, then K3 sts from the cable needle
c6b	cable 6 back: slip next 3 sts onto cable needle and hold at back of work, K3, then K3 sts from the cable needle
c8f	cable 8 front: slip next 4 sts onto cable needle and hold at front of work, K4, then K4 sts from the cable needle
c8b	cable 8 back: slip next 8 sts onto cable needle and hold at back of work, K4, then K4 sts from the cable needle
c12b	cable 12 back: slip next 6 sts onto cable needle and hold at back of work, K6, then K6 sts from the cable needle
dec	decrease
foll	following
folls	follows
g	grams
in	inches
inc	increase
K	knit
K2tog	knit 2 stitches together
LH	left-hand
mb	make bobble: knit into front, back, front, back front of next stitch. Turn work and purl the 5 stitches. Turn work and knit the 5 stitches. Slip the 2nd, 3rd, 4th and 5th stitches off over the 1st stitch. Pull firmly on yarn to tighten bobble

mm	millimeter
oz	ounces
P	purl
patt	pattern
pb	place bead: thread beads onto yarn before starting to knit each section: (RS and WS rows): with yarn on RS of the work, slide bead up yarn, slip 1 stitch purlwise, if necessary bring the yarn between the needles to work the next st, leaving bead in front of slipped stitch
ps	same as the instructions for pb, replacing a bead with a sequin
P2tog	purl 2 stitches together
P3tog	purl 3 stitches together
rep	repeat
RH	right-hand
RS	right side of work
st/sts	stitch/stitches
sl	slip
sl1p	slip 1 stitch purlwise
t2b	knit into the back of the 2nd stitch on the left-hand needle, then knit into the front of the 1st stitch, then slide the 2 stitches off the needle together.
t2f	slip the next stitch onto a cable needle and hold at front of work, K1, then K1 from the cable needle.
t4lr	slip next 3 sts onto cable needle and hold at back of work, K1, put 3 sts back onto left-hand needle, P2, K1
WS	wrong side of work
yb	take yarn back between the needles
yf	bring yarn forward between the needles
yon	take yarn over needle
yfrn	bring yarn forward and round needle
*	repeat instructions between * as many times as instructed

Acknowledgments

My sincerest thanks go out to the following people who together made this book possible: Michael Wicks for his beautiful photographs; Emma Callery, for her fine editorial skills; Marie Clayton, at Collins & Brown for initiating the project; Luise Roberts, for her tremendous support and for her wonderful charts; Rowan Yarns, for their continuous and generous support, especially Kate Buller and Ann Hinchcliffe; Marilyn Wilson, for her careful pattern checking; my fantastic group of knitters who worked day and night to complete the projects – Heddy Abrahams, Jenny Still, Julie Cox, Eleanor Yates, Heather Esswood, Liz Jenks, Ann Yockney, Michele Cooper, Helen McCarthy and Marie Edwards; Kate Buller for the photographs in the techniques section; and my dad, who again willingly transported me and my knitted projects to wherever we needed to be, whenever we needed to be there!

Debbie Abrahams: www.da-handknits.demon.co.uk

SUPPLIERS

USA
Westminster Fibers
4 Townsend West
Suite 8
Nashua
New Hampshire 03063
Tel: (1 603) 886 5041 / 5043
E mail: mail@westminsterfibers.com

Australia
Australian Country Spinners
314 Albert Street
Brunswick
Victoria 3056
Tel: (03) 9380 3888

Canada
Diamond Yarn
9697 St Laurent
Montreal
Quebec H3L 2N1
Tel: (514) 388 6188

Diamond Yarn (Toronto)
155 Martin Ross
Unit 3
Toronto
Ontario M3J 2L9
Tel: (416) 736 6111

UK
Rowan Yarns
Green Lane Mill
Holmfirth
West Yorkshire HD9 2DX
Tel: 01484 681881
www.knitrowan.com

Suppliers of beads

USA
Rowan Yarns and Jaeger Handknits (see contact details under yarn suppliers)

Mill Hill
PO Box 1060
Janesville, WI 53547-1060
www.millhillbeads.com

UK
Rowan Yarns and Jaeger Handknits (see contact details under yarn suppliers)

Beadworks (mail order)
16 Redbridge Enterprise Centre
Thompson Close
Ilford
Essex IG1 1TY
Tel: 020 8553 3240

Beadworks
21a Tower Street
Covent Garden
London WC2H 9NS
Tel: 020 7240 0931
www.beadshop.co.uk

Creative Beadcraft Limited (mail order)
Unit 2
Asheridge Business Centre
Asheridge Road
Chesham
Buckinghamshire HP5 2PT
Tel: 01494 778818

Ells and Farrier
20 Beak Street
London
W1R 3HA
Tel: 0207 629 9964

Suppliers of buttons

USA
Rowan Yarns and Jaeger Handknits (see contact under yarn suppliers)

UK
Rowan Yarns and Jaeger Handknits (see contact under yarn suppliers)

John Lewis department stores.

Suppliers of sequins

UK
John Lewis department stores.